When we looked through this book we wondered, "Why didn't we think of that?" There are so many great ideas we don't know where to start! *Connect with Your Grandkids* is a must-read for grandparents who want to energize their relationship with their grandkids.
—GARY AND NORMA SMALLEY
Founders of Smalley Relationship Center

What a great collection of stories, tips, insights, and fun-filled ideas on how to support, love, and be a positive spiritual influence in our grandchildren's lives. We all need ideas for what to do with our grandkids that will be fun and make wonderful memories—and this is the book. I'm so glad Cheri said, "Just be yourself." I got a paper and pen and started writing down the things that clicked with my personality. I couldn't put the book down—I got so energized, I wanted to do it all!

Thank you, Cheri, for taking the time to gather and pass on to us all this great information from so many grandparents, as well as your own experiences.
—FERN NICHOLS
Founder and President, Moms In Touch International

Once again, Cheri Fuller is ministering to families with a great resource. This book is for today's grandparents who are passionate about their grandchildren but need practical, inspiring ways to solidly bond with them. I have eight grandchildren eight years old and under, and I can't wait to get started implementing ideas from Cheri and other fabulous grandparents.
—DENISE GLENN
Founder, MotherWise Ministries and Kardo International Ministries

Sign us up! Cheri Fuller has taken away all excuses for being uninvolved grandparents. She has given us a treasure trove of ways to bond with those wonderful grandkids.

Whether you were as effective as you wanted to be as a parent, grandparenting offers all of us a chance to once again groom a generation for greatness. It's not often we get such a significant second chance. *Connect with Your Grandkids* gives us hands-on ways to make this a reality.

Grandparenthood is far more than rocking chairs. It is a second chance to do all of the "ought-tos" and "should-haves" that the busyness and demands of daily parenthood kept us from doing. With her practical, hands-on suggestions, Cheri Fuller has done all of the hard work for us. Now the fun can begin!

—TIM AND DARCY KIMMEL
Authors of *Extreme Grandparenting*
Founders of Family Matters

What a privilege grandparenting is! And a great principle that we use daily is to begin with the end in mind: How do you want your grandchildren to remember you? As fun? Interested in them? Joyful? Creative? A great storyteller? Encouraging? When we connect from our hearts and are deliberate in making the most of every opportunity by making activities fun and lighthearted for them, relationships are grounded in love and become life-changing places of refuge for the grandkids—and even more so for us as grandparents.

If you've ever asked "Now that I'm a grandparent, what do I do?" read this outstanding book you're holding and not only will you know what to do next, it will also show you how to become a real family champion. It is both practical and life changing.

Absolutely every grandparent needs a copy of this book! Grab a copy for yourself or give one to a grandparent in your life. Way to go, Cheri—your book is outstanding!
—DR. GARY AND BARB ROSBERG
America's Family Coaches
Founders of The Great Marriage Experience
Speakers, authors, national radio-program co-hosts

connect with your **grandkids**

FOCUS ON THE FAMILY

FocusOnTheFamily.com

A Focus on the Family Resource Published
by Tyndale House Publishers, Inc.

connect with your
grandkids

fun ways to bridge the miles

Cheri Fuller

Tyndale House Publishers, Inc.
Carol Stream, Illinois

Connect with Your Grandkids
Copyright © 2009 by Cheri Fuller

A Focus on the Family book published by
Tyndale House Publishers, Inc., Carol Stream, Illinois 60188

Focus on the Family and the accompanying logo and design are federally registered
trademarks of Focus on the Family, Colorado Springs, CO 80995.

TYNDALE and Tyndale's quill logo are registered trademarks of Tyndale House
Publishers, Inc.

Editor: Kathy Davis
Cover design by Erik M. Peterson
Cover photograph copyright © by PhotoAlto/Eric Audras/Jupiter Images. All rights
reserved.
Interior design by Lois Keffer

The author is represented by the literary agency of Alive Communications Inc.,
7680 Goddard Street, Suite 200, Colorado Springs, CO 80920,
www.alivecommunications.com.

Library of Congress Cataloging-in-Publication Data
Fuller, Cheri.
  Connect with your grandkids : fun ways to bridge the miles / Cheri Fuller.
    p. cm.
  Includes bibliographical references and index.
  ISBN 978-1-58997-536-1 (alk. paper)
  1. Grandparenting—Religious aspects—Christianity. 2. Grandparent and child—
Religious aspects—Christianity. I. Title.
  BV4528.5.F85 2009
  649'.10853—dc22

Printed in the United States of America
2 3 4 5 6 7 8 9 / 15 14 13 12 11 10

Also by Cheri Fuller

Dedication

*To my parents, George and Mildred Heath, who,
though their lives were short, loved their children and grandchildren
dearly. And to my parents-in-law, Jack and Joan Fuller (Mimi),
who loved our children and grandchildren well.
As the only living grandparent, Mimi,
you've been the grandest great-Mimi of all.*

*And to my grandchildren,
Caitlin
Caleb
Noah
Luke
Josephine
and Lucy,
I wouldn't be Nandy without YOU!
You light up my life!*

Contents

Acknowledgments

It's been a joy to write this book and meet some of the most awesome and creative people I've ever talked to, from east to west, north to south. When I became a grandparent, I didn't have a grid to follow. My grandparents were quite old by the time I came along, and we were such a big bunch of children—six in all. So when the time came, I was eager to learn from other grandparents; it's been quite a learning curve! I was inspired by Mom, who was a praying and involved grandma to her 22 grandchildren until she died at age 59. And I'm immensely grateful for sweet Mimi, our beloved only grandparent, and Lynn and Dru, the greatest great-aunts in the world.

I would like to extend a heartfelt thanks to all the grandmas and grandpas who shared their experiences and ideas—especially Peggy Powell, Cheri Potter, Phyllis Stanley, and Janet Page, who planted the seed for a grandparent book in my mind years ago. Thank you to all those who prayed as I wrote this book: dear Janet, Peggy Stewart, Peggy Powell, Betsy West, Glenna Miller, Doris Little, Kathy Wirth, Cynthia Tonn, Susan Stewart, Corrie Sargeant, Cynthia Morris, Patty Johnston, and Jill Miller.

I'm so grateful to have a great editor in Kathy Davis, and to Larry Weeden who caught the vision for my book. Thanks to Focus on the Family and Tyndale House Publishers for the opportunity to once again partner with you in building families and encouraging parents and grandparents!

Chapter 1

The Joy of Connecting with Our Grandchildren

*Grandchildren are very special.
Perhaps that's why they are called "grand"
children. And we grandparents are
"grand" to them too.*
—Dick Ayers

I waved good-bye to my daughter-in-law as she carried our three-week-old grandbaby Josephine through security to an American Airlines jet; it would take them across the country from Oklahoma to Bethesda, Maryland, where they would meet our son Chris and settle into their new home. As I prayed for their safety and protection, I also whispered a prayer: "Lord, help me connect heart to heart with Josephine, even though she's going to live so far away." Little did I know that a year later they would move even farther away, across the ocean to Hawaii where her dad was assigned to serve as Battalion Surgeon for the Marines. From there they would eventually move to Wisconsin.

A few years later, our oldest son and his wife packed their Explorer and two more of our grandchildren, Caitlin and Caleb, and moved away to Cincinnati, Ohio. Two years later they would move on to St. Louis. Because they'd spent the first few years of their lives only 15 minutes from us, we had enjoyed wonderful times together and developed a great bond of love. Now they too would be in another state. Waving to them as they drove out of the driveway, I prayed, "Lord, help me stay connected to these sweet grand-kids, even though they'll be 13 hours away." God has graciously answered that prayer by giving me many creative ideas and crossing my path with some special grand-parents who shared their experi-ences. With God's help I've built loving relationships with my grandchildren, who now number six—three girls and three boys—and range in age from eleven years old to two: Caitlin, Caleb, Noah, Luke, Josephine, and Lucy.

> "Where does your grandma live?" "Oh, she lives at the airport. And when we want her we just go get her. Then when we're done having her visit, we take her back to the airport."
> —an eight-year-old

Spanning the Distance

Like me, millions of Baby Boomers have become grand-parents with families scattered across the country. Baby Boomers now comprise over 30 percent of the population. These grand-parents may be busy with careers, travel, and activities of their own, but they want to connect with their grandkids, make memories, and be a loving influence despite geographical sepa-ration. I've talked with grandparents all over the nation as well as overseas who share a great bond with grandchildren in faraway places. A wise person once said that it doesn't matter where you live, it matters who you are. How encouraging that our prayers can span the geographical distance between ourselves and our grandchildren and build a legacy of love that bridges the genera-tions! The sweet memory of times together and encouraging words can last a lifetime.

It's the Little Things

One of the best things I've learned from interviewing other grandparents is that it's the little things done consistently and lovingly that build a great relationship—not just the big splash! In this book, you'll find plenty of those little things, in addition to touching stories and quotes on the value and blessing of being a grandparent.

Whether it's using a webcam to read a bedtime story, making small, personalized photo albums to take home after a visit, sending e-cards to share your interests, or taking a trip together, this book is full of practical ideas for building relationships with your grandchildren, whether they live down the block or across the country.

Different Sizes and Ages

There are all kinds of grandparents. We come in different sizes, ages, shapes, and life situations. Grandparents today seem younger than grandparents did in the past due to better health and a more active lifestyle. I've met some terrific grandparents in their 70s and beyond who are still actively involved in their grandchildren's lives.

There are first-time grandmas who are so overjoyed about their darling, smartest-kid-in-the-nursery grandchild that they bring out a brag book at every opportunity. Some grandparents have been blessed many times over and find themselves spread a bit thin keeping in touch with all their grandchildren, but love them just the same. Others have teenage grandsons and granddaughters who are in the midst of difficult situations quite different from anything the grandparents encountered at that age.

> A child is born only once, but a grandparent is reborn with each new grandchild.
> —Joan Holleman

Some grandparents live near enough to pick up their grandchild once a week, which makes bonding easier. Others have three sets of grandkids living in three different parts of the country, which makes building relationships more challenging. Some are single and some are married. There are grandparents who have lots of money to take their grandchildren on lovely trips. Others have more limited budgets, but do a great job of connecting with their grandkids in their own backyards. Some grandparents are retired and have lots of time to travel across the country to visit their grandchildren. Others are busy with a career, full-time or part-time, but still want to be a blessing to their grandsons and granddaughters.

> They make my spirits soar!
>
> —Jackie Kennedy Onassis on her grandchildren

You may be Poppy and Wa Wa or Mimi and Gramps, Oma and Opa (German-Dutch names for grandparents), or Nana and Boompa. Some of the most fun grandparent names I've heard are Tootsie and Pops and Honey and GranDan. My husband and I are called Nandy and Poppa because that's what our first granddaughter decided to call us. I know a Ga-Ga and DuPah and Nonny and Papps. Then there's Ama White Car; Ann's twin grandboys creatively designed that name for her and it stuck. That takes the cake!

No matter what name we're called or how different we are, there's one thing we all have in common: a desire to connect with our grandchildren! That's why you picked up this book. We want to love them and be a support and positive influence in their lives.

Let me assure you, grandparents are not obsolete! They hold an important place in the life of every family. Families have changed: There are more divorces and an increased number of single moms (and dads). This trend greatly affects grandparent-ing, and sometimes brings step-grandchildren into our lives. Because families are more mobile than ever, with frequent moves for corporate or military assignments, there's more long-distance grandparenting. Children today are often plugged-in and over-scheduled, which presents yet another challenge in trying to build a relationship.

This is especially true of teens and preteens. As we know from raising kids, it can be challenging to connect with older kids. Their world is expanding rapidly and they may likely be more interested in their friends than family members—even you, their beloved grandparents! But if you've built a relationship when they were young and continue to keep in touch occasionally by e-mailing, dropping a card by snail mail, or sending short text messages, they'll feel your love and support across the miles. It will make a difference in their lives even if they don't tell you so right now. As someone once said, we can either be a port in the storm or a part of the storm. How much better to be a support and offer your 'tween and teen grandchildren your unconditional love and an open door at your home—that is, when they can find a little space in their planners for you!

It's a difficult time to be raising children. The pressures on today's families are increasing as parents struggle to balance work with family. There are stresses and threats to children's well-being that didn't exist when we were raising our children: school violence, Internet predators, pressure to perform, and substance abuse at very young ages, to name just a few.

That's why grandparents are needed more than ever—not only to support fatigued parents, but also to be life-givers who provide a much-needed sense of stability, security, and unconditional love. We can make a tremendous difference in the lives of our grandsons and granddaughters, whether they are two or eighteen, simply by believing in them and staying connected.

What Kind of Grandparent Will You Be?

You can be any kind of grandparent you choose to be! There are Cookie-Baking Grandmas whose creativity is best expressed in the kitchen; they love to involve their grandkids in making bread, cinnamon rolls, or homemade pizzas. There are Artsy Grandparents who share their interest in art and crafts with their grandchildren.

There are Reading Grandmas, like Linda Zachry, who wrote me this note.

My husband and I live in Dallas, Texas, but my granddaughter lives with her parents in Redondo Beach, California. Despite

the distance, I see Paige at least every three months and she
already loves for me to read books to her. I've shared classics like
Goodnight Moon, Pat the Bunny, Noah's Ark, *illus-*
trated by Peter Spier, and The Little Engine That
Could. *I love being a reading grandmother.*

I recently met a spunky, 5'2" Marathon Grandma who is 67
years old and just completed her 50th marathon in three years—
one in every state in the U.S.! Her 10-year-old grandson has
started joining her in 10K kids' races. This shared experience
has built a great connection between them.

There are Outdoor Grandparents like me and others I
know who enjoy nothing better than taking bike rides, going to
the zoo on a sunny day, or taking the grandkids fishing for the
afternoon. (When it comes to fishing, I'm talking about
Grandpa, not me!) For some grandparents, the best way of connecting is taking the children on an annual camping trip. I've
even met Teaching Grandmas who hold Spanish or etiquette
classes for their grandchildren.

There's the Power-Visit Grandma who doesn't get to see
her grandkids very often. When she does, it's a whirlwind of fun
and activities. The Theatrical Grandparent writes plays for her
grandkids to perform at Christmas and other special occasions.
One of my personal favorites is Patty, the Zany Grandma, who
tinges her beautiful white hair with pink just because she enjoys
it (her grandsons do too).

My sister Marilyn is a hands-on Science Grandma who
helps her little grandson Decker launch rockets in his backyard.
When she visits, she brings fascinating items such as bug catchers
to trigger Decker's curiosity.

Although grandmas often initiate activities with the grandkids, grandfathers can also have a positive impact and build
wonderful relationships with their grandchildren. Grandpas are
just as important in the family dynamics! Here's what a six-year-
old had to say about his grandpa, my husband, Holmes.

He's my Poppa.
He's awesome and he shares with us.
When I visit, Poppa lets me sit in his
  big red comfy chair.
He's real friendly and drives real good.
I love Poppa!
                              —*Luke, age 6*

You'll choose your own unique role as a grandparent. There are no rules saying you have to fill a certain role or be all of the above. Get "out of the box" of preconceived notions about what grandparents should be. Be yourself!

It's not the role you play, but the love you invest in your grandchildren that makes the difference. Avoid unreasonable expectations that come with trying to be everything to your grandkids, or comparing yourself to other grandparents. This is not a competition. Every grandparent has something unique and valuable to offer. Often it's the simple, homegrown activities that make the best memories.

The Blessings of Being a Grandparent

Investing in our grandkids brings tremendous blessings. They light up our lives. Maybe your teenage grandson drives you during the snowy season when the roads are icy, as Patty's grandson does. Perhaps you get calls from a granddaughter that brighten your day, or a serenade from a toddler grandson who sings *This Little Light of Mine* via webcam.

Your experience might be like that of Shirley Utz who, during chemotherapy, received encouraging e-mails like this one from her 10-year-old grandson, Hunter.

If you got this in the morning, it's Happy Hunter! Can't wait to come to TEXAS and see you! I didn't know hugging makes your hormones healthier but soon I'm going to give you a big hug. They put the port in—cool! I can't believe you are so calm about this! You have a fun, special, wonderful, glamorous day!
                              Love, Hunter

Our grandchildren's love for us enriches our lives immeasurably. As Barbara, an Oklahoma grandma, expresses, "It's been a wonderful journey. I wouldn't give the world for the joy I've had being a grandma, and being invited to be involved in my grandchildren's lives now that they are teens and grown-ups. You just get one shot at it, so take the time when it comes. They grow up so fast!"

Loving Our Step-Grandchildren

In our nation, many marriages end in divorce. That means that many grandparents will have one or more step-grandchildren come into their lives. Getting to know and love your step-grandchildren can be one of the best things you'll ever do; it will certainly make a huge difference in their lives.

To step-grandchildren, you're just their grandparents. Susan shares:

> *I never thought of my grandmother as a "step." She was Grandma Pape, my dad's stepmother. I looked forward to spending a couple of weeks each summer with her and my Grandpa Pape all by myself. These were the fondest childhood memories I have. They lived in Indiana and I was six hours away in Ohio. I don't know at what age I realized she was not "blood" but a step-grandmother, but I never gave it much thought. It was all about her love for me and the love I saw between Grandma and Grandpa. She was my grandma and I was her granddaughter and I never looked at our relationship as anything but that. In fact, I actually thought having more grandparents than my friends had was pretty cool. She was a gift to me and I am forever thankful that she was an integral part of my life.*

After the shock wore off when Frances Strickland's son and his girlfriend announced they were getting married in three weeks, the Stricklands realized they would soon become step-grandparents to two-year-old Caitlyn. Frances and her husband believe that love is a commitment, not a feeling. They set their hearts on loving their daughter-in-law and her child whom they'd seen only a few times. On Caitlyn's third birthday, Frances wrote this letter.

> *Mimi met you for the first time in May before you turned two. Little did I know that in less than six months you would become my precious little granddaughter. My first thoughts of you were that you had beautiful brown eyes that sparkle and dance and that you were very smart. At two you could pronounce any word clearly and count to ten. Your mom came here to dress for the garden wedding in our backyard, and I attempted to get you down for a nap beforehand. I'll never forget that I told you I loved you and you responded with, "I love you." I was blessed that during the wedding you chose to sit on my lap. Caitlyn, you are such a sweetheart, and I'm so glad God placed you in our family. To know you is to love you, and I do—with all my heart.*
>
> *My love, Mimi*

Love, acceptance, and being included in special activities with other grandkids can go a long way toward helping step-grandchildren through the changes and losses they've experienced. They may be slow to warm up, especially if they are adolescents. Or they may be very close to their other grandparents. But research shows that step-grandparents who are patient and accepting can have meaningful, loving relationships with their step-grandchildren. This book suggests scores of ways for step-grandparents to connect and build good relationships with the precious ones who've come into their lives.

Believing in Your Grandkids

No matter what obstacles children face, they can become great adults if they have someone who believes in them and loves them no matter what. That someone is often a grandparent.

I love the story of Luciano Pavarotti, one of the world's greatest opera singers, and the effect his grandma's love and encouragement had on his life. When he was a little boy, his grandmother scooped him up into her lap and said, "You're going to be great . . . you'll see." Pavarotti's mother wanted him to be a banker, but he took a different direction—teaching elementary school and singing occasionally. His father urged him to quit teaching and study music; at age 22, he did. He became an insurance salesman so he'd have time for voice lessons.

Although Pavarotti credited his father for steering him back to music, he credited his grandmother as being the real source of his inspiration. "No teacher ever told me I would become famous. Just my grandmother."

What's Ahead

For all of us, the grandparent-grandchild connection is a work in progress. In this book you'll find terrific tips and insights to help you along the journey. You'll read about creative ways to connect through letters and packages, through storytelling and sharing family history, through cooking, through photos and memory albums, and through webcams and technology.

You'll gain helpful ideas on handling the sometimes puzzling issue of gift-giving and how to make memory albums that connect your grandchild to the rest of the family. One chapter focuses on how to share your interests and plug into things that fascinate your grandchild. Another deals with making the most of visits with grandkids, at your house or theirs. Plus, you'll be inspired by just-for-fun activities to do with your grandsons and granddaughters.

One growing trend in families is "Cousin Camps" held in the summer at grandparents' homes or at a cabin. After interviewing a number of energetic grandparents who host Cousin Camps, I'll share the best tips on having a fun, stress-free time with all your grandkids together. And I'll offer great advice for planning a Grand Sleepover with one or two grandkids.

I hope you'll pick and choose, using the ideas that work for you and your lifestyle. Tweak these suggestions to make them your own; let this book be a springboard. Working on this project, I've gathered more ideas than this grandma can use in a lifetime, so save some ideas for later! The good thing is, I won't ever run out of ways to connect!

You don't have to read the chapters in order. If you have interest in a particular topic, go to that chapter. For example, if you're tech-challenged and want some ideas on how to connect with your techy grandkids through the Internet, go to Chapter 9. If you want to share family history through storytelling, see Chapter 13. If you want to have Grand Sleepovers, check out Chapter 4.

You'll find some activities that require financial resources; others cost almost nothing but the investment of your heart and time. If you like "easy," you'll find lots of ideas that require little or no planning. If you're up for more challenging activities, you'll find those as well. The pages ahead are packed with years' worth of creative ways to keep in touch, express your love, and make memories with your grandkids, whether they're down the street or a continent away.

Are you ready for a great adventure? You can build a wonderful connection with your grandchildren, and this book will show you how.

> **Our daughter in North Carolina used to say**
> we only visited her to see our grandsons and she took second place. To some degree, she was right! We thoroughly enjoyed raising our own children, but grandchildren awaken a different kind of love that's hard to explain. My three grandsons—Bryan, Andrew, and Eric—are my treasures and the light of my life.
> —Anne Basile

Chapter 2

Sharing Your Interests and Theirs

The best thing to spend
on your grandchildren is time.
—Unknown

When you share a skill or special interest with a grandchild, you never know how far he or she may go with it. Karen O'Conner, in her book *Innovative Grandparenting*, tells of a grandma who was an amateur photographer. She had been taking pictures for decades, and had even won an award for one of her photographs. She gave her grandson Graham a camera for his 10th birthday. From then on, the two of them went on photo shoots to take all kinds of pictures, from parades to portraits. Graham now dreams of a career in photography.

Karen also tells about Roger, a teenager whose granddad was a Civil War buff, a real repository of stories about the rivalry between the Confederacy and the Yankees. Granddad got Roger a subscription to the Historian Book Club. Now that they share many books on American history, Roger has engaged with great enthusiasm in his high school history courses.

Sharing our hobbies and skills provides terrific opportunities to bond with our grandchildren. Something special happens when two people bike together, knit together, or participate in any other hobby together. Think of your running partner or your quilting group. There's a special connection, a closeness that springs from partnering in an activity. Not only does sharing of interests provide a great point of connection, it may also inspire children to develop special interests of their own.

Amy Krupka, a young woman I interviewed, told me about the great impact her grandparents had on her by sharing their skills during a special week at their farm. They taught her, along with her sisters and cousins, about gardening and entertaining.

> *My grandfather always had a large vegetable and fruit garden plus a few flowers to make my grandmother happy. Daily he weeded, pruned, or fertilized. If we wanted to spend any time with him, it was always in the garden, early in the morning before he left for work, or after five o'clock when he returned home. Most Saturdays he spent in the garden harvesting and thinning the fruits, vegetables, and flowers. He taught us how to start a hothouse with a few bricks and an old window. We worked right beside him, because we thought it was a treat.*

Amy's grandmother shared her gift of hospitality with Amy and the other grandchildren. Originally from Europe, her grandma brought the tradition of entertaining guests for afternoon teatime or evening coffee and cake almost daily. Before she was 10, Amy loved making cut-flower arrangements for the table. She'd learned how to set the table correctly with a platter of cookies, serve their guests, answer the door, and clear the table. By the time the grandkids were 12, they felt very grown up as they set up the percolator, unplugged it, carried it to the dining room, and served coffee to 8 to 10 people without spilling a drop. Amy says:

> *We learned about hospitality from Grandma because it was a way of life for her. Sometimes she was expecting people, but many times they just showed up. She taught us to be gracious and diplomatic and enjoy the visit. I always learned so much just listening to their grown-up conversations.*

As a mother today, what Amy learned as a child has transferred into how she welcomes people into her own home. She's grateful for all the practical life skills she learned from her grandparents. And, because of the time she spent with her grandfather in the garden, she has the greenest thumb in the neighborhood!

But it wasn't all work at the grandparents' house; they did fun things, too. Her grandparents enjoyed card games and taught Amy and her cousins every single game they knew so everyone could join in. They played Crazy Eights, Sevens, Hearts, War, Uno, Black Jack, Rummy, Solitaire, and a variety of board games. When the children were young, the grandparents let them win about 50 percent of the time. As the grandchildren grew older, they had to learn strategies to win. All the grandchildren enjoyed the games, and learned from their grandparents how to win and lose graciously. When Amy was 10 years old, her grandma taught her to crochet. Now in her forties, Amy still has a passion for crocheting and is teaching her daughter and her daughter's 10-year-old friend.

Each of us has skills we can pass on to our grandchildren. Maybe you think that your skill is not that unique. The truth is that you have talents and skills that will benefit the younger generation. Passing on your skills is a special gift you can give your grandchildren. Kids usually like to do what the grown-ups are doing; they love having a chance to join in.

Pat Rowe, a Texas grandma, teaches Spanish to her grandchildren when they visit. My husband Holmes shares his love of caring for birds with our grandkids. He lets them help fill the bird feeders and put water in the birdbath. He bought them binoculars to watch the birds during rare still moments. Since Poppa is a builder, he also helps them make birdhouses from wood scraps.

A Fort Worth granddaddy loves to work with wood and metal. Together he and his grandkids have made wooden airplanes, metal men out of pipe, and step stools to help little ones reach the sink. When the children arrived, their first question was always, "Granddaddy, what can we make?" And when it was time to split wood for the winter, they got involved at their level of ability.

One grandma offered etiquette classes for a few weeks over the summer break when her granddaughters came to stay with her. She taught lessons in grace, beauty, good table manners, and proper social behavior. Knowing how to conduct themselves in social situations built their confidence and self-esteem. Many years later, those granddaughters fondly remember Grandma's etiquette lessons and how they benefited from her instruction and involvement in their lives.

An Ohio grandma and grandpa took their grandsons fishing in mountain lakes and streams. In Florida they went fishing and crabbing in the ocean. Lakes and oceans soon became their grandkids' favorite places. One moonlit night, these grandparents watched the boys catching minnows for bait. When they went fishing off a jetty the next day, the grandsons became too absorbed to take a break for lunch. When called in for dinner, they insisted on making "just one more cast." They straggled in later with sheepish grins. Though empty-handed, they were ready to go again the next day. Albums filled with fishing trophies illustrate their later success as memories were built year by year.

> **My Grandma Barrett was a talented lady.**
> She was a seamstress, a singer, a poet, farmer's wife, and mother of three boys, among many talents. I got to stay with her for a week every summer and she helped me gather eggs, bake potato rolls, pick berries, and thread shoestrings through empty spools. I especially enjoyed making hollyhock flower dolls and clothespin escorts.
> —Bonnie Kruizenga

Sharing Your Travels

Judy Douglass has the privilege of traveling around the world frequently as the publications and women's resource director of Campus Crusade worldwide. In each country she visits, she picks up a little something for each of her three grandchildren. The only one old enough to really appreciate these travel treasures so far is Madison, age six. When Judy returns home with Madison's gift, she tells a little about the place she visited and the people who live there.

One of Judy's favorite finds came from spending a month at the beach on sabbatical. Over that month she gathered a variety of shells to begin a collection for Madison. She also bought a book on shells; then she and Madison looked up all the "houses" she'd collected and the creatures that lived in each one. The shells gave them an opportunity to talk about all the different creatures and people God has made, and His love and provision for each.

> My Grampa Bradley took me on some wonderful adventures. He taught me a lot—fishing, hunting, and work. He let me help him plant and water trees when I was four. He covered up holes he'd encouraged me to dig, so people wouldn't drive a car into them. He taught me how to spade a garden, mow a lawn, and trim it properly.
>
> —Michael Enzi

Before my husband and I left for speaking engagements in South Africa and Zambia, I made a notebook for each set of grandkids and sent it to them. I titled the first page *NANDY & POPPA GOING TO AFRICA*, and added a colored map of the country as well as our photos with all the grandchildren. At the bottom of the page I placed pictures of zebras and long-tusked elephants. The second page contained a description of Zambia with a small map, coat of arms, and basic information from Wikipedia, the free Internet encyclopedia, including geography, history, flowers, culture, languages, and the kids' favorite section—the native animals of that country. I did the same for South Africa.

When we returned, we brought each grandchild a hand-carved hippo or giraffe bought from locals in the bush country of

Zambia. We shared photos and gave them copies to put in the notebooks. We also shared a few travel stories, such as the time I was petting lion cubs in a game reserve and one cub reached out and tried to grab my purse!

Are you're interested in foreign countries? Even if you can't travel abroad, you can take an imaginary trip with your grandchildren. When you get together, let them help pick the place they'd like to "go." Whether it's China or New Zealand, Mexico or Africa, get a map and read about the destination. Check out a travel video or book about the country from the library. Prepare and eat a meal of the native food and pretend you're there. You can go some place new each time your grandkids come to your house. With a map of the world, you can keep track of where your imaginary travels have taken you by putting a star sticker on each place. Your grandkids will delight in learning about other parts of the world. And since kids love imaginary play, they'll have a wonderful time without leaving home!

> I like to connect with the grandchildren in the vegetable garden. They help me plant, tend, and harvest a winter and summer garden. We take lots of pictures through the process so the grandchildren can see the different stages the garden is in, whether they're with us or not.
>
> Often character lessons come from tending the garden. For example, we planted snow peas this past fall, but they didn't have fruit until March. We talked about having lots of green vines and beautiful flowers in our lives, but no fruit. We then asked God to bring the bees so the fruit would come forth, and within a week the fruit came…we had a very nice crop of snow peas.
>
> —C. J. Kirkpatrick

Grand Science Adventures

My sister taught meteorology and chemistry at the high school level for many years. Naturally, she enjoys sharing her love of science through hands-on activities with her four-year-old grandson Decker. When he was three, she brought him a Stomp Rocket on one of her visits. They assembled the base, stomped on the launcher, and watched the foam rocket fly up 200 feet in the air. Decker was thrilled, and they launched more rockets.

This summer she brought him a ladybug habitat. They read a book about ladybugs, and the ladybug larvae arrived in the mail before her visit ended. Long after her visit, Decker will continue growing ladybugs, watching them in their colorful habitat, and talking about them with Ga-Ga via webcam. When the ladybugs have grown up, he and Mommy will let them fly away in the garden.

Because Anne Abernethy, my friend from college, finds ants interesting and knows there are lessons we can learn from these hard working creatures, she took an ant habitat to her grandchildren. They delighted in observing the busy ants digging their tunnels.

Besides ant farms, you can find all kinds of wild and crazy science kits for your grandchildren to explore to their hearts' content. Looks for "atomic worms," beetle barns, butterfly gardens, and live frog habitats. If science is your cup of tea, one of these science kits might be just the thing to share with your grandkids. Besides browsing children's learning stores, you can Google hands-on science kits and find scores of fun science possibilities.

A Night at the Opera: Sharing a Love of Music

Maybe you don't get excited about insects. But perhaps, like Susan French and me, you love music. Susan noticed that the opera, *La Traviata*, was going to be performed at the Arizona Opera Company in Phoenix, not far from her home. Susan decided to take her nine-year-old granddaughter Ella and one of her little friends to their very first opera. Before going, she explained that "La Traviata" means "the trivial" and gave them an overview of the story so they could follow the performance. She told them that it was a sad story about a flirt named Violetta whose life had been filled with trivial and meaningless things until she fell in love with a very nice man at a party. They had an interesting discussion about the girls' take on the trivial things in their lives, as well as what was really important.

Because they bought tickets just before opening night, they got the last seats in the house—the last row of the balcony. Susan thought the girls might be sad that they were so far away from the stage. Quite the contrary—they thought it was cool to be all dressed up and sit so high that they could see the whole glorious scene from their amazing vantage point: the fantastic orchestra, the stage and performers, and all the elaborate set designs. Above the stage was a screen with English subtitles, so the girls could follow the plot.

After the first act, Susan noticed that there were empty seats in the front row, and thought Ella and Annika might like to move. They were given permission to change seats and enjoyed the last two acts of this dramatic performance from the very front row. Susan worried that the last sad scenes, in which Violetta coughs blood into her handkerchief before dying of tuberculosis, would be too much for the girls. But they were mesmerized by the drama and singing and loved it. As they enjoyed dinner after the performance, Susan asked the girls how they liked the opera. They answered, "It was so wonderful and beautiful! But we liked the whole view from our balcony seats the best." Susan hadn't accounted for the fact that kids often bring a different perspective. What a great reminder that God might be giving our grandchildren special insights. Sometimes we're the ones who learn from them!

Susan felt honored to take Ella and her friend to their very first opera and to share a special conversation after the perform-

> You share the same interests as your grandchildren—naps, for instance.
>
> —Willard Scott

ance. Sharing the music she loved with her granddaughter made a meaningful connection—and who knows? Maybe Ella will become a lover of opera when she grows up!

Music connects people. When we share a love for a particular kind of music with a friend or family members, it becomes common ground. Music is one of the best stress-relievers in our crazy-busy, stressed-out world. Here are some ways you can share music with your grandkids.

Take them to live musical performances: concerts, children's symphony programs, or an opera as Susan did. Most towns have live musical theatre, kids' matinees at the symphony, and other concerts that can introduce children to the beauty of live musical performances.

Share a lullaby. Sharing music can begin when your grandchildren are babies. Whenever I visited my littlest grandchildren and was putting them to bed, I sang a song my Papa sang to me when I was a child. I call it, "Papa's Lullaby."

> *Sleep, baby sleep;*
> *close your bright eyes,*
> *and I will sing to you*
> *a tender lullaby.*

Each of my six grandkids knows this song because it got passed down in the family, not only from me but from their parents to whom I sang it when they were babies. So they call it "Nandy's Song."

Sing whenever you put the little ones to bed. You may not think you have a good voice, but it is sweet to your grandchildren. Nursery songs, lullabies, and folk songs are good choices to build a bridge of music from our generation to the next.

Teach young grandchildren simple songs and let them join in. Sing together on the phone or when you are with them. It could be a special song you make up with their names in it.

Kick up your heels. Put on folk music or tunes from the '60s and '70s, and dance to it together.

Introduce them to classical music. Play classical music while your grandkids draw. Give them big sheets of paper, watercolors, markers, or crayons, and let them draw up a storm as they listen. There are wonderful recordings of classical music especially for children. Some of my favorites are the award-winning CDs and DVDs of the world's top classical composers such as *Beethoven Lives Upstairs*, *Mr. Bach Comes to Call*, and *Mozart's Magic Fantasy.* These are wonderful to play in the car or at bedtime.

Kids love music and delight in making music themselves. They can lead the band, playing the part of the conductor, while grandma and grandpa play instruments. We can help them make rhythm instruments and encourage them to play along to different kinds of music. Making and using instruments is a fun activity for a cousins' camp or a sleepover with younger children.

Children from the toddler stage
to early elementary school like to keep the beat as they march and move to the music. Learning to keep a steady beat and practice different rhythms is an important foundation for later success on an instrument. And it's lots of fun! You can buy sets of rhythm instruments or make your own.

Maracas: Put rice or beans in plastic spice jars for easy musical shakers.

Percussion instruments: Pots and pans with a wooden spoon, or, for a quieter drum that's easier on the ears, make one out of an oatmeal box.

Rhythm sticks: Two wooden dowels from the lumberyard or hardware store, or two pieces of garden cane (bamboo).

Melody bells: Sew bells on elastic for kids to wear on their wrists.

Sharing Your Grandkids' Interests

It's always a great investment to carve out some time to spend with individual grandchildren and share in their interests. There's a lot we can learn from our grandkids. When we're open to what fascinates them, we find opportunities to connect on their turf.

Think about what your grandchild enjoys, then choose an activity involving that interest that you'll both enjoy. It doesn't have to be expensive or elaborate. I find that the best connecting times flow naturally from my grandkids' unique interests.

For example, my granddaughter Josephine loves crafts. When I go to see her in Wisconsin, I often bring a craft for us to create together. When I spent a week with Josephine in early December to help with her new baby sister, I brought an already-put-together gingerbread house on the airplane with me. Good thing, because I am not good at putting gingerbread houses together; I wanted to focus on the fun of decorating it. After arriving in Milwaukee, I went to the grocery store and bought gumdrops, small candy canes, tubes of red, white, and green icing, and other sweets. Now this may sound elaborate, but trust me—it wasn't. My artistic four-year-old granddaughter Josephine took the lead and knew just how she wanted to decorate the gingerbread house. I was her helper elf! We took pictures along the way, complete with icing on both of our faces, and had lots of fun.

My grandboys enjoy throwing the football in the yard. From playing with my two boys who are now dads themselves, I throw a mean spiral to the three grandsons. I do creative writing with Caitlin, my 10-year-old granddaughter. We write "color poems" or "Scar Stories" together. She reads me the newest stories she's written and I share my love of writing with her.

I entered into six-year-old Noah's current great interest in football cards by making him a notebook for his collection. He had brought the football cards over one day and expressed his sadness that he couldn't find his Tom Brady/Patriots card and some other favorites. They'd gotten lost because they were in a pile in his room. I got a white, three-ring notebook from my office. I made a cover that said *NOAH'S FOOTBALL CARDS* in giant red letters, printed it out, and slipped it behind the clear plastic on the cover. Next I got some clear sports card sheets from Al's Sports, the local trading and buying store for sports cards. And voilà! Noah had a great place to organize all his cards, and we have a good point of connection that's ongoing. He loves to drop by the sports card store and pick a card or a pack of cards.

This interest spread to his brother Luke, who wanted a football card notebook of his own. Then Caitlin and Caleb, two

---

Skills and Interests to Teach Grandkids

Think: What do I know that my grandkids' parents don't know or don't have the time to teach them? If you haven't engaged in a hobby or interest in a while, you may want to get books from the library to help you brush up on specifics. Consider this list of interests and skills to share.

- ✳ photography
- ✳ creative writing
- ✳ knitting and crocheting
- ✳ woodworking
- ✳ gardening
- ✳ fishing, hunting, and rock climbing
- ✳ scrapbooking
- ✳ stamp or coin collecting

---

more of my grandchildren, wanted to trade sports cards with their cousins.

My grandkids got me interested in watching *American Idol*. Wherever we are, most of us watch it. When we can, Noah and Luke come over for an *American Idol* finale night, or I go to their house. I fix popcorn and serve apple juice and cookies to make it fun. This year during the results show, they wanted to connect with their cousin Josephine in Wisconsin via webcam to talk about the performances and see who she thought would win.

All six of my grandchildren are real music lovers with quite a wide repertoire of favorite music, from Johnny Cash and U2 to Coldplay, *Hannah Montana*, *High School Musical* tunes, Jack Johnson, and Leona Lewis.

You too can create a great connection with your grandkids by sharing the things you love with them and being willing to hear about the activities and ideas that excite them.

Just-for-Fun Stuff to Do with Grandkids

*You never forget how to smile
when you have grandchildren.*

—Unknown

Let's face it: One of the great things about having grandchildren is the fun stuff we get to do together that makes us smile. We don't have all the responsibilities we once had as parents, such as carpooling and making sure our kids did their homework and brushed their teeth. With our grandkids, we can do things just for fun—and then send them home to their parents!

From tea parties to treasure hunts, night walks, and water gun fights, there are lots of inexpensive activities that make marvelous memories. The just-for-fun activities in this chapter are things you can do when your grandchildren come to your house to visit, during sleepovers and Cousin Camps, or when you visit their homes. Please don't tackle all these things in one visit! But when you need something quick, you're bound to find a great idea in the pages that follow.

Little Girls and Their Tea Parties

One of my favorite activities is a tea party. From the time our oldest granddaughter Caitlin was two years old, we had "Muffy Bear Tea Parties" together. I put a little round tablecloth on the floor and got out the miniature tea set that my mom had given our daughter Ali when she was young. We made tiny little muffins or cookies for the Muffy Bears— which, of course, were eaten by Caitlin! Even though she's 10 years old, Caitlin still enjoys making and eating treats for the Muffy Bears and having teatime with Nandy.

Whenever our granddaughters Josephine and Lucy come from Wisconsin to visit, I get out the basket of clothes for all the Muffy Bears. The girls dress the bears, and sometimes a few dollies, in party outfits. They arrange the bears and dolls sitting up on our tablecloth and in doll chairs I found at a garage sale.

> If becoming a grandmother was only a matter of choice, I should advise every one of you straight away to become one. There is no fun for old people like it.
>
> —Hannah Whitall Smith

When the mini muffins are ready, Josie pours the "tea"—water or apple juice—for each bear and doll, and we pretend that the bears just love their treats and tea. But we know who enjoys the treats most of all.

Sheila, a grandma I met via e-mail, has a fun story about stuffed animals attending tea parties. After raising three boys, Sheila became "Gran" to two darling little girls. Tea parties are a tradition whenever Kate and Kennedy come to her house. Their favorite thing is making the fun tea party food. They frost miniature marshmallows and animal crackers, eat "finger sand-wiches" (directions follow), and use food coloring to make "green tea." Each tea party has its own special theme.

One of Sheila's favorite memories is of a garden tea party they held on a summer morning. They sat on a large blanket in the grass with a bouquet in the middle—handpicked from Gran's garden. Before they sat down, Kate asked if George could come. Her Curious George was twice as big as her three-year-old body, but he was welcome, and she served George a generous portion. A wonderful time was had by all.

Is your granddaughter in another state or country? When Cheri Potter was teaching in an international school in Thailand, she and her granddaughter Audrey (in Kansas) learned how to have a pretend tea party over the phone. She taught Audrey to say, "Hello Madame, would you care for tea?" Then they talked through how many lumps of sugar and how much cream they wanted, and spoke of cucumber sandwiches, and dessert.

Audrey decided that one of their "transatlantic pretend parties" would be a luncheon. She served her grandma the expanded menu for the day that she created herself: pizza, popcorn, and peanut butter and jelly sandwiches; for dessert, pie and vanilla ice cream. Then Audrey presented her with the "bill," which she said was one penny. From tea parties and luncheons, their pretend play developed into a full-blown three-course meal, and later, a drive around town and trip to the zoo and the mall. These tea parties required no toys, dolls, or props. All it took was a little time and imagination. And kids have much better imaginations than we adults do!

> Don't leave out the boys! Even little grandsons might enjoy pouring tea in teacups and making fun food for the party. Mine have asked to join the tea party when they saw the goodies. They even brought their own Webkins.

Does your grandchild have a collection of Webkins, favorite bears, or dolls? Ask who she'd like to invite to the tea party. On one occasion, you could have a fairy tea party complete with fairy dust cookies—sugar cookies sprinkled with sparkling sugar. Another time, hold an English high tea. Use your best china to serve cucumber sandwiches and scones with whipped cream and jam. A picnic-style outdoor tea party is ideal in the spring or summer, and nothing's nicer than a Christmas teatime with holiday cookie cutter-shaped sandwiches. Let the grandchildren help you decide what kind of tea party to have next! In Chapter 12 you'll find more ideas on creative treats to make together.

Ideas for Tea Party Treats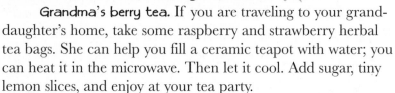

Grandma's berry tea. If you are traveling to your granddaughter's home, take some raspberry and strawberry herbal tea bags. She can help you fill a ceramic teapot with water; you can heat it in the microwave. Then let it cool. Add sugar, tiny lemon slices, and enjoy at your tea party.

Tea party essentials. Gather some brightly-colored sugar sprinkles, colorful pre-made icing, green food coloring, animal crackers, mini-muffin tins, and miniature marshmallows. Having these tea party essentials on hand will make preparation time simple and fun. Let your grandchild put colorful frosting on mini-marshmallows and animal crackers for one tea party. Next time, make bite-size cookies from refrigerated sugar cookie dough and add "fairy dust" sprinkles before baking.

Finger sandwiches. Use a hand-shaped cookie cutter to make a great finger sandwich. Kids love cutting the bread with the cookie cutter and filling it with peanut butter and jelly.

Fruit pies. Use doll-size pie pans to make little pies with your grandchild. Press refrigerated dough in the pans. Add chopped apples and sprinkle with sugar, small pats of butter, and cinnamon.

Bubbly Strawberry Lemonade. With only three simple ingredients, this makes a very special, refreshing, bubbly drink for tea parties and teddy bear picnics! Your grandkids will love stirring the ingredients as you pour them into a pitcher.

> 2 quarts of sparkling water or club soda
> 1 12-ounce can of thawed lemonade concentrate
> ½ cup strawberry puree, blended from 1 cup
>   frozen strawberries
> ice cubes

In a large pitcher, mix thawed lemonade concentrate, sparkling water, and strawberry puree. Let your grandchildren stir to combine. Chill until party time. Pour over ice in tall glasses. Pop a whole strawberry in each glass to look extra festive!

Scones for kids to make. Warm scones, served just as they are removed from the oven, are an English tradition for teatime. Here's an easy recipe that your grandkids will enjoy making with you. Using whipping cream to replace the butter and egg that some recipes call for will streamline your preparation so little bakers can have fun!

1½ cups all-purpose flour
⅓ cup sugar
2 tsp. baking powder
½ tsp. salt
½ cup whipping cream
2 tsp. finely shredded lemon peel
whipping cream and sugar to garnish

Preheat oven to 375°.

1. In a large mixing bowl, combine flour, sugar, baking powder, and salt. Make a well in the center of the flour mixture. Add the whipping cream and lemon peel.

2. Stir until the mixture is crumbly. Put flour on little hands, then knead the dough, roll it, and pat it in a ball. Turn the dough onto a lightly floured surface.

3. Pat the dough into a seven-inch circle. Use a table knife to cut the dough into six or seven wedges. Place the wedges about one inch apart on an ungreased cookie sheet. Mark them with a "T" for teatime. Brush lightly with cream and sprinkle with sugar.

4. Bake about 18 minutes or until golden brown. Serve warm with your favorite jam.

Heartfelt Ideas and Low-cost Activities ✳

These simple ideas make for happy experiences and fond memories.

Make a dress-up box. That old hope chest full of things like the white gloves you wore to your prom, jewelry, old hats, and your tiara from the homecoming queen pageant can be a source of fun and magic for your grandkids. Just get the chest out and let them peruse your treasures from the past. Or, fill a box with dress-up clothes from garage sales, costumes purchased at 75 percent off after Halloween, props, and hats. The dress-up box will spark many happy hours of imaginative play.

Hop on bubble wrap. Save your bubble wrap that comes as packaging. Kids of all ages love to jump on the bubble wrap and hear it pop. This is great for getting the wiggles out on a rainy day.

Hula hoop contest. If you don't have an old hula hoop, you can purchase a few very inexpensively at a discount store. When my grandkids visit, they love to have a hula hoop contest—indoors if it's a cold or rainy day, and outside if it's sunny. The person who swings the hula hoop the most times wins. Boys and girls get into this activity, and so do I—it's great exercise for my waist and a good way to get their wiggles out!

Sweet sculptures. Give your grandchild toothpicks and gumdrops to make creatures, characters, and structures.

Genius kit. On a rainy day, give each grandchild a bag filled with 10 to 20 of the same items: pencils, teaspoons, spools, or household goods. Using only these items, challenge the children to design something that can be used for a purpose, such as a hammer, measuring stick, or whatever they dream up.

Show night. When all our grandkids were together this summer, we had a family potluck dinner and then what the kids call "Show Night." Show Night included performances by all the grandkids. Even the youngest grandchild, Lucy (20 months), got in the act and danced to the music. They all got their chance to be the star. We had a stand-up microphone and all the kids brought their CDs for backup. They created their own costumes, with Josephine and Caitlin wearing long blonde Hannah Montana wigs and Noah dressing like one of the Jonas Brothers. Luke and Caleb were rock stars and Caitlin was the emcee. The audience—their parents and grandparents—loved it. For the last song, we were all invited to dance. What fun we had.

Treasure hunt. When Luke, my five-year-old grandson, came over to spend the night recently, I had a treasure hunt all prepared for him. Kids love surprises, and Luke is no exception. Since he loves pirate stories and pirate stuff, we made it a pirate treasure hunt. He wore a black patch over his eye as he started the search. I gave him hints and remarked, "You're cold, you're getting warmer," until he was under the couch and found the first clue. Since Luke is learning to read, he had fun decoding the clues, and I helped him decipher them. If your grandchild is a pre-reader, you could use pictures for the clues. Here are some treasure hunt clues. This is not an attempt to share fancy poetry —which it's definitely not!—but to stir up your own ideas.

⭐ *CLUE 1*
Inside the place where videos are kept,
You'll find another clue
That will help you find your treasure
And lead you the right way too.

⭐ *CLUE 2*
Under the play kitchen
Waiting for you
A clue may be hiding
Just see and do!

⚹ *CLUE 3*
Look where the birds eat
And you will find
The last clue waiting
And you won't mind.

That message, which didn't rhyme at all, led to the last clue—my favorite reading chair. Luke liked the treasure: a little box filled with balloons, a lollipop, gum, and a one-dollar bill. Though the box was filled with simple things, he jumped for joy and wanted to do another treasure hunt. I made up new clues and off he went.

Special names. One grandma and grandpa gave each grandchild a special adjective to go before their name, just for fun: Happy Hunter, Awesome Dawson, and Sweet Skylar. It made a connection of endearment that bonded their hearts; the grandparents are the only ones who call them by their special names. In the Phillips family, everybody has a special name. The grandkids' nicknames are Little Lady Bug, Bittybug, Doodlebug, and Love Bug. The children don't say Grandma, but Grammiebug! Grammiebug's other half isn't merely Grandpa, but "Papa Pirate," in honor of the fact that he once pretended to be a pirate. The fun nicknames create a strong connection even though the grandparents live in North Carolina and grandkids live in Florida, Pennsylvania, and Colorado.

Granny's magic bag. One of the most fun ideas I've heard and put into practice is Granny's Magic Bag. Buy any kind of gaudy, beaded, glamorous-looking bag. Think of the kind of bag a magician would use in his stage act. Cheri Potter (who shared this idea with me) found her Granny Bag at a weird '70s store; I found mine in the night market in Chiang Mai, Thailand, while on a mission trip there. Your local discount stores and flea markets have tons of possible bags to choose from.

What's in Granny's Magic Bag?

Here are some things you can put in your Granny's Magic Bag to delight your grandkids.

- ⭐ a small, bright-colored high bouncing ball
- ⭐ sticks of sugarless bubble gum
- ⭐ an engaging mini-book you can read them
- ⭐ a tiny pack of crayons and notebook
- ⭐ funny socks
- ⭐ a magnifying glass (take it to the park and look at what's hiding in the grass)
- ⭐ a musical toothbrush to use when a grandchild is visiting your house
- ⭐ a finger puppet
- ⭐ a pack of flower seeds you'll plant together in the garden
- ⭐ small sticker book
- ⭐ inexpensive novelty bracelet
- ⭐ small goodies
- ⭐ a mini travel game

Fill your bag with little things like a tiny sticker book, little stuffed animals, or a small notebook and crayons—anything to occupy your grandchild for 15 to 30 minutes. Take the bag with you when you go someplace together. When your grandchild gets restless or is cranky at a restaurant or during a long car ride, quietly say, "Wow...I guess it must be time for something...from Granny's Magic Bag!"

I have tried this idea with my grandkids. Trust me—they love the element of surprise and always look forward to getting together again to see what's in Granny's Magic Bag. Yours may be "Nana's Bag" or "Mimi's Bag," but it's all for pure fun and the magical element of surprise.

Bubble-blowing fun. When it comes to entertaining your grandkids, silly things can be the most memorable. In a time when more and more complex electronic toys are marketed to children and even babies, there are plenty of simple things that still bring a smile to their faces. Blowing bubbles is one of those things. To make easy, jumbo bubble blowers, bend a coat hanger without a kink at the top into a circle and dip it into a flat pan full of bubble mix. Or take a plastic six-pack soda pop holder, dip it into the solution, twirl it around, and your grandchildren can make lots and lots of bubbles.

Pour the bubble mixture in a big bowl (preferably on the patio or driveway) and let the children go wild with a straw or colander. Bubble fun is easy, inexpensive, and makes great photo opportunities.

> Mix together gently until combined:
> ¼ cup liquid dishwashing detergent (Joy, Ajax, and
>   Dawn are best)
> ¾ cup water
> 1½ Tbsp. light corn syrup
>
> For longer-lasting bubbles, add a few teaspoons of glycerin. Store in an airtight container. Let mixture sit for a few hours before blowing bubbles. Enjoy!

Water gun play. Recently, I asked my friend Connie about the most fun activity she'd ever done with her grandkids. She instantly replied, "Playing with water guns." On a trip this spring to see their almost-two-year-old grandson, Ethan, they picked up three one-dollar water guns—one for Ethan, one for grandma, and one for grandpa. Although they also brought

Ethan several new books and a rather elaborate kid swimming pool that cost a bundle, the cheap water guns were by far the biggest hit, as was the ensuing water gun fight with his grandparents. As they ran around the backyard taking aim with their plastic water guns, Ethan's giggles turned into belly laughs. Now whenever they visit, he asks, "Where are the water guns? Let's play!"

Ice cream for breakfast. A chapter about fun stuff wouldn't be complete without having ice cream for breakfast. At home, the grandkids' parents strive to serve healthy, well-balanced breakfasts. We grandparents do too, but sometimes—why not have ice cream? Ask each grandchild what his or her favorite flavor of ice cream is. Then buy it, label the cartons with their names, and put them in the freezer. If they don't get to come visit often, small cartons work best. Then when it's ice cream time, they have their own special flavor that nobody else gets to eat!

Holiday fun. Holidays are great times to kick up our heels and have fun. There are myriad holiday-themed activities for grandkids. Here is a sampling of ideas for the Fourth of July and Christmas.

⭐ Frances and her friend have a Wee Fourth of July parade and festivities to allow the visiting grandkids to get to know the neighbors. This year will be their seventh annual party, and the number of participants has grown to 80! They start by decorating bicycles, scooters, and wagons in patriotic themes with red, white, and blue balloons, and sparkly streamers. They do patriotic face-painting and collect goods for servicemen and women's care packages. They parade twice around their circle and come back for a potluck lunch, with everyone contributing. After lunch come the games: limbo, a pinquata (a water piñata since they live on a lake), scavenger hunts, obstacle courses, a Jell-O eating contest, and water balloon races. Each year they add a new game to the mix. Afterward they enjoy watermelon and watch the fireworks across the lake—a perfect end to a fun day! What sweet memories this Fourth of July event has made for their grandchildren.

✵ One of my favorite things to do when all six grandkids gather at Christmastime is to have two gingerbread houses prepared. The first year, I learned my lesson: It took me so long to bake the sides and top of the house that the icing slid off and the whole thing collapsed! So now I buy them already put together. I put out bowls of gumdrops, red hots, M&Ms, and tubes of different-colored frosting, plus two big tubes of white frosting to edge the house and roof. All this goes on a long table covered by a plastic tablecloth. The children form two teams and have a great time decorating the houses, chatting, and dipping into some of the candy. When they're finished, we glue cotton batting on the heavy cardboard backing to look like snow and use the gingerbread houses for our Christmas table decoration.

Because every one of our grandchildren is unique, some activities in this chapter may be a hit and kids will beg to do them again and again. Others may not be as popular. Just move on to Plan B and try something else. Whatever you choose, this just-for-fun stuff will fill your grandkids' hearts with unconditional love, laughter, and cherished memories.

Have a ball!

Our two oldest grandsons

lived three and a half hours away when they were young. At that time we lived on a farm. Farm living was an easy way to connect with them during their visits. We hiked all over the place, went fishing, rode four-wheelers, collected eggs, and fed the sheep. Now we live in town and have four grandchildren close by. I take my little grandsons on four-wheeler rides on a regular basis. They count on me to come by and pick them up when we're out checking on the farm. Last spring we took them on a one-day vacation to explore caves. We are fortunate to live near caves that are open for expeditions, even for little ones.

—A Grateful Granddad

Grand Sleepovers

Home is where my
grandkids are.

——Unknown

A favorite among grandkids is what I like to call "Grand Sleepovers." Whether it's spending the night at the grandparents' house, camping out in a tent in the backyard, or bunking in a hotel together, the fun begins when the children wave good-bye to Mom and Dad. Then out come the sleeping bags, board games, and popcorn, and the adventure begins. Simple moments shared during your grandchild's sleepover will quickly become fond memories.

Our grandson Caleb, age seven, spent the night with us this spring. After dinner together, Holmes and I watched Caleb skateboard on our hill. We threw the Frisbee and kicked the soccer ball until dark. Then we played games inside: Candyland and Zingo, which is like Bingo only with superheroes. By the time we got to Connect Four, Poppa had fallen asleep reading his newspaper, so I read Caleb a book about Daniel Boone. The next morning, we made a trip to the Dollar Store, a favorite spot of Caleb's. He picked out an FBI team kit, dark glasses and handcuffs included, for—you guessed it—one dollar! Holmes found some scrap lumber, so when we got home, Caleb's morning activity with Poppa was making a wooden shield and sword.

They also chopped wood together and Caleb got to hold a real Civil War rifle and a World War II Japanese samurai sword. What a big deal for the grandsons! We didn't do anything fancy or travel farther than a few miles, but it was a memorable time.

Having just one grandchild at a time for a sleepover not only gives us a chance for fun, food, and games, but allows us to know and understand that boy or girl more deeply. It provides time to hang out and eat Popsicles in the summer, or sit by the fire and read a book in the winter. It's special to have all six grandchildren here at the same time; that happens only twice a year. Because they are so close in age, I feel like a P.E. teacher trying to corral them! So I cherish our one-on-one times together.

A Twin Sleepover

From the time Ann's twin grandsons, Max and Oliver, were very small, she would have them over to spend the night. Granted, she had her hands full with the double fun of identical twin boys, but they had a blast. They might eat in or go out for hamburgers, then make a craft or paint a picture. Max and Oliver would play outside with the neighbor kids. The last activity of the evening was always watching a movie together, and the movies often had a theme.

For example, on the 100-year anniversary of John Wayne's birth, the three went to Sam's Club and bought several videos of John Wayne's movies to watch together. Another night was a baseball theme; they had hot dogs for dinner and watched *Field of Dreams*. They've had musical theme nights when they watched *Oliver*, and the boys danced along with every production number. If they were interested in a particular actor, Ann rounded up other movies that featured that person.

> ### Sleepovers with my grandparents
> were very special, because it was one of us at a time—there were eight grandkids, four boys and four girls. Time alone with my grandparents was precious. We got to relax,

garden, and crochet together. Many times they told stories about when they were growing up, how they came to this country with only a trunk and no English, and how they met and married. I wouldn't trade anything for those sleepovers and special times together.

—Amy Krupka

But the fun didn't stop there. When all three of them climbed in her king-sized bed and the lights went out after story time, Ann would look over at her angelic-looking grandsons, thinking they were asleep. Inevitably one of the twins would begin to whisper, tell a joke, or giggle. The chuckles were contagious and pretty soon they'd all end up laughing until tears ran down their cheeks. Even though they're now 12 years old, Max and Oliver will still pick a Grand Sleepover over other activities. These are memories Ann will never forget.

Just Together Times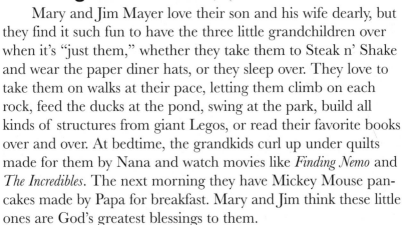

Mary and Jim Mayer love their son and his wife dearly, but they find it such fun to have the three little grandchildren over when it's "just them," whether they take them to Steak n' Shake and wear the paper diner hats, or they sleep over. They love to take them on walks at their pace, letting them climb on each rock, feed the ducks at the pond, swing at the park, build all kinds of structures from giant Legos, or read their favorite books over and over. At bedtime, the grandkids curl up under quilts made for them by Nana and watch movies like *Finding Nemo* and *The Incredibles*. The next morning they have Mickey Mouse pancakes made by Papa for breakfast. Mary and Jim think these little ones are God's greatest blessings to them.

Girl and Boy Sleepovers

Doris, an Illinois grandmother, has 15 grandchildren ranging in ages from 19 months to 15 years. Each family leads busy lives with work, school, church, and sports activities. And she's busy too. But she feels it's very important to have special times just for the grandchildren. Their favorite way to do that is to have sleepovers—one just for the boys, seven of them, and one just for the seven grandgirls. The baby, 19 months old, is too young to make the sleepovers.

My memories of my Nana

are very vivid. Despite having 17 grandkids, she had a special talent for making each of us feel that we were her favorite. She never visited without bringing her signature gift, a box of Cracker Jacks. To this day I can't see a box of Cracker Jacks without thinking of Nana. She never forgot a birthday or a special holiday, and she was always sending notes.

When we (eight of the grandkids) lived in Wisconsin, she would drive all the way from Tulsa and rent a hotel room with a pool and have a pizza party and sleepover for us—no parents allowed. It was something that we looked forward to every year.

But it wasn't what she gave us or what she did that resonates with me; it was who she was. Nana had a great sense of humor and loved to laugh. She cultivated a personal relationship with each of us and encouraged us to seek out each other as well.

When I went to college, I got a card in the mail from Nana with $20 and instructions to call my cousin Tim and go have lunch with him. She wanted us to maintain ties in our family. Even when we were adults, nothing pleased her more than hearing of cousins meeting to hang out.

—Maggie Fuller

The activities and games vary according to their ages, and sometimes there is more than one thing going on. Here's a sampling of what they do: Inside, they play board and card games like Scrabble, Settlers, Sequence, Blurt, Apples to Apples,

Racko, and Old Maid. Outside, they roast marshmallows over the open fire, and the older kids play "Ghost in the Graveyard," which is a "Hide and Go Seek" game at night.

Sometimes they all go to the zoo, the county fair, a local dairy farm, or out for ice cream. For a special outing, they take the train to downtown Chicago and go to Navy Pier, the Lego Store, or Build-a-Bear, topped off by eating at the Rain Forest Café.

They wind down later at night with popcorn and a movie; their favorites are VeggieTales, *The Road to Redemption*, and the Chronicles of Narnia series. The kids like to sleep together in the same room in sleeping bags, and the grandparents aren't too fussy about when they go to bed. By midnight they're all sound asleep. The next morning they're up early asking for Grandpa's pancakes, and one of the grandchildren will offer to read the devotions.

When the kids pack up after lunch, Doris reminds them not to be cranky when they go home or their parents might not allow them to come back to spend the night! For the last two years, they've had an end-of-school celebration sleepover for all the grandchildren—that's 14!—on the last day of the semester. And each child also gets a birthday sleepover, alone, or with one or two cousins. They get to choose a favorite place to go and a favorite activity.

Museum and Zoo Sleepovers

A few times a year, many zoos, science museums, and children's museums hold overnight activities where grandparents and grandkids get to do things behind the scenes they could never do during the day. They can take a night train tour at the zoo to see prowling lions and tigers, take a flashlight tour of Egyptian mummies in an historical museum, or make popsicles for polar bears. At some planetariums, once a quarter children can sleep under the stars and hear stories of the constellations. And at children's museums they get to listen to bedtime stories by professional storytellers. Check with your local museums and zoos to see what nighttime programs are available.

Themed Sleepovers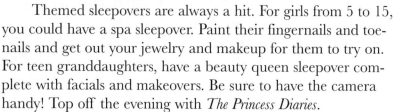

Themed sleepovers are always a hit. For girls from 5 to 15, you could have a spa sleepover. Paint their fingernails and toenails and get out your jewelry and makeup for them to try on. For teen granddaughters, have a beauty queen sleepover complete with facials and makeovers. Be sure to have the camera handy! Top off the evening with *The Princess Diaries.*

For a princess theme, let your granddaughters make their own princess crowns with cardboard and glitter. They can use scarves and pillows to create a throne, then help you stir up a "feast" for the royals to eat.

When Judy and Ann, Oklahoma grandmas whose grandchildren live in Beirut, Lebanon, flew over for a visit, they planned a princess-themed sleepover at the hotel where they were staying. They invited their little granddaughter Anna to spend the night. They brought Cinderella costumes complete with glass slippers for Anna, and boas and feathered hats for themselves. They swam in the "royal" hotel pool and had a tea party with fancy cookies and pastries. They read princess books and even went downstairs in the hotel restaurant in their costumes to have dinner—despite the other peoples' stares.

> **Our girls love to go for night walks**
> when they spend the night, and Mimi always has some glow sticks on hand for the adventure. On the last night walk, the girls were having playful sword fights as they meandered through the dark woods and down by the lake. They gazed up at the stars. They discovered the bones of a deer, and their Poppy explained what the different bones were. At Christmas one year as we took a night walk, we wound up singing Christmas carols to a neighbor who waved to us. For our family, night walks are a special part of sleepovers.
>
> —Frances Strickland

They pretended their hotel room was a magic castle, and Anna played to her heart's content. At bedtime, they cuddled in the bed and watched a *Cinderella* DVD. When the grandmas flew home, they left the princess costumes and movie for Anna to enjoy, along with lots of special memories.

For boys, you could plan a superhero sleepover. Here are some ideas to spark your imagination. Make capes out of fabric to tie around their necks, play Zingo, then watch a favorite superhero DVD.

For a pirate sleepover, get eye patches, pirate makeup, and costume items at dollar and discount stores so kids can dress the part. Go to a nearby playground and let your grandkids pretend they are on a pirate ship in the ocean, or place a big board over two concrete blocks in the back-yard to let them "walk the plank." Later, show *Peter Pan* or *Hook* for younger grandboys, or the first *Pirates of the Caribbean* movie for older ones. Be sure to tell pirate stories before the lights go out.

> You don't need to be a super grandma for your grandkids to cherish you. One treasured memory can last a lifetime.
> —Janet Lanese

For little children, create your own Disney sleepover. Get some Donald Duck, Goofy, or other Disney character costumes when they are marked down 75 percent after Halloween. With the kids in costume, lead them in a parade around the house. Later, have a Disney movie marathon for winding-down time and the next morning have Mickey Mouse pancakes topped with whipped cream. Mickey Mouse pancakes seem to be quite a trend when grandkids spend the night—whether it's on the east coast, west coast, or middle of the country.

A craft sleepover means getting out the clay or foam visors and stick-ons, or setting out the beads to make jewelry. A craft sleepover is great before Christmas because you can make holi-day ornaments. There are lots of arts and crafts projects in Chapter 11 that you can choose from.

It's great when you have a tent and can go camping in the backyard. But a camping sleepover doesn't have to take place outdoors. You can have an indoor campout by putting up a small tent in the family room or making a tent out of blankets or sheets. Put lots of pillows inside, then cook your dinner and marshmallows for dessert in the fireplace. Go on a "bear hunt" with flashlights in the backyard or inside the house with all the lights turned off. Top the evening off by telling stories when the children are tucked into their sleeping bags.

Tips on Not Just Surviving but Enjoying Sleepovers

Maybe when one grandchild comes over to spend the night it's a piece of cake, but inviting all of them, or even half of your energetic boys or girls, may sound daunting. Whichever you choose, here are some ways to enjoy a grandchild's sleepover and make it "Grand."

Keep it simple. Remember that simple moments when you're just having fun together make happy memories. It's not about doing expensive activities or eating fabulous food, but about making connections and enjoying each other.

Try some silly stuff. Whether it's blowing bubbles or having a Silly String war, do something just for the fun of it. See Chapter 3, "Just-for-Fun Stuff to Do with Grandkids," for lots of ideas.

Cook together. Let your grandkids help you in the kitchen. You could make a pizza or cookies from refrigerator dough. Let them top the pizza or decorate the cookies. Be sure to take pictures during the messiest part of the process!

Make a craft. With a big roll of white paper and markers, your grandkids can make a mural or draw to their hearts' content as you chat and catch up on their lives. Check out Chapter 11 on arts and crafts for lots of simple and inexpensive ideas.

Create a welcoming place. Hugs, acceptance, and smiles let children know they are welcome at your house. So does having playthings on hand. Get some dress-up costumes and old clothes, board games from garage sales or the discount store, and balls for outside play. Designate an area of their own where these toys, games, and costumes are available—and where they don't have to worry about messing up your house.

> Nobody can do for little children what grandparents can do. Grandparents sort of sprinkle stardust over the lives of little children.
> —Alex Haley

Set boundaries. For example, running is for outside, not in the house; eating happens in the kitchen, not in the living room. Every household has its own guidelines, and the sleepover will be more fun for all if the kids know these in advance.

Organize. If you're having several grandchildren at a time for a sleepover, it's best to have a game plan. But instead of going at a frantic pace during the whole visit, leave time to just relax and hang out together.

Get some rest before the grandchildren arrive so you'll be sure to have plenty of patience and energy.

Whatever kind of sleepover you plan—simple or more elaborate, on your turf, theirs, or at a hotel—it's all about making memories and enjoying the time together. And just think, you have the whole rest of the week to catch up on your sleep!

Connecting Your Grandkids through Cousin Camps

*Fun is always just around
the corner
when you have grandchildren.*

—Unknown

For Barbara Erwin's grandkids, Cousin Camp started many years ago when there were only two grandchildren. Since the boys lived in different states, she invited them to come without their parents for a week to her home in Enid, Oklahoma. Pretty soon they had three grandchildren, then four and five, so every year Cousin Camp grew. After eight years, the sixth and seventh grandchildren came along. The grandchildren couldn't wait to reach four years of age so they could join the camp adventures.

How did these grandparents manage to have a bunch of grandchildren at their house for a week and not pull out their hair? Barbara's philosophy was always making memories by doing simple things: making a lemonade stand, playing croquet in the backyard, playing basketball games in the driveway, climbing trees, making mud pies, and having picnics and water gun fights where Meme and Grandpa got wet too. Grandpa even gathered wood and helped the grandchildren build a fort in the backyard. And since Grandpa was a naval captain, these grandparents took advantage of free or low-cost activities on the military base nearby.

This was one organized grandma! She always made a plan before her grandchildren arrived, and the kids got to make choices about the activities. They picked what they most wanted to do based on their ages and interests. But the great part was that everybody got to play and participate.

When there were only two grandchildren at a time, it was easy to find a bed for them. But as the number grew, there weren't enough beds in their small house to accommodate them all, so the kids slept on pallets. It never mattered, because the cousins loved bunking in the same room.

Barbara and her husband bought bicycles at garage sales so whenever the grandchildren came for the camp week, they each had their own bike to ride. Since one grandchild lived in a large metropolitan area and another lived in a mountainous area with no flat places to ride, biking was one of the highlights—they got to enjoy freedom they didn't have at home.

Barbara always had a Plan A for days when they could go outside for activities, and a Plan B for rainy days. A Plan A day started with a bike ride to the local convenience store. They peddled down to the store like the Pied Piper and his band, Grandma in front, then the grandchildren, youngest to oldest, bringing up the rear. Each child had a little cloth bag Meme had made that attached to their handlebars. With the one dollar it held, the kids got to buy whatever candy they wanted and put it in their bag for the ride home. Back at Grandma's house, they loved to get out their stash of candy and swap with each other.

A Plan B day included things like going to museums, shopping at the mall, going to the movie theater, or playing Chinese checkers, Chutes and Ladders, Wahoo, and Monopoly. Barbara took the cousins back to places where she grew up, and told them stories about her childhood adventures.

A young, energetic grandma in her forties, Barbara was a school administrator who had the summer off. She looked forward to planning and implementing Cousin Camp. Her husband still worked, so he was involved in the evening activities: mini-golf, go-carts, and snow cones every night. As the boys got older, when PaPa Jerry got home, they would head for the golf course.

> In a society where everyone is moving at the speed of light, grandchildren slow us down, allowing grandparents a respite from our treadmill existence. The quick smile of a four-year-old grandson jumping into your lap, the loving hug and kiss of a granddaughter, or a serious conversation, golf, or chess match with a maturing grandson can make even the busiest company chairman or CEO stop and enjoy the moment.
>
> —Archie Dunham

Cooking took a backseat to fun, so they ate out every night and had picnics at noon. Though Barbara was a fastidious housekeeper, during camp week she let everything go. The focus became being with the grandkids and having a fun, memorable time—not keeping a spotless house. She knew she'd have time for cleaning up after they'd gone home.

Now these young people are either teenagers or in their twenties, yet when they get together, they still talk about their memories from Cousin Camp, and how it bonded them. They're spread around the country but still close to each other and to their grandparents. They all agreed that going to the grandparents' each summer was like going to Disney World. Though what they did at Cousin Camp wasn't expensive or exotic, they wouldn't have missed it for the world.

Cousin Bonding

Whether you call it Cousin Camp, Nana's Camp, or a creative title like Ju-Ju Camp, inspired by the name the cousins call you, there are great reasons for gathering all your grandkids together in one place for a few days or a week of fun. Besides enjoying the company of your grandchildren without their parents, one of the major purposes for these camps is for our grandchildren to connect and build relationships with each other. Since many of our grandchildren live in different parts of the U.S. or even in different countries, a week spent together builds memories and rapport between cousins that can last a lifetime.

When Julie Jordan's grandkids were very young, she started inviting them to spend a week at her home in Kerrville, Texas. She single-handedly loaded them in a big van for a week of swimming, playing tennis, and later, golf. For six years she took nine grandchildren—with no helpers. What a gal! If they were potty trained, they got to go.

During the first camp week, the youngest granddaughter, who was three years old, said, "Grandma, we're having hot dogs for lunch? I don't like hot dogs!" Julie said, "Look, honey, this is a camp and everybody eats the same thing at camp." The nine-year-old piped up, "Then let's name our camp 'Camp Oakland Hills!'" Everyone liked the name so much that after naptime,

---

I love being with everybody!

All of my cousins live in a different part of the United States so I rarely get to do anything with them. Having the adventures of staying at Mimi and PaPa's house, at a resort, going on road trips, and just telling jokes under the covers at night, I will always remember cousins' camp and my wonderful MIMI and PAPA!

—Jaclyn Adams, age 11

---

they all headed for town and had "Camp Oakland Hills" T-shirts made. The moms contributed by preparing casseroles and sending them along for each night's main meal.

In addition to all the fun, Julie made a chart with chores for the grandkids to do. Those grandchildren are all grown up now and spread around the U.S. and the world; they live in Brazil,

Indonesia, Seattle, Washington, D.C., Dallas, and Austin. But all have stayed close through the years, and this Labor Day they planned to fly in to see each other and their grandma.

Different Grandparents & Different Cousin Camps 🍁

I'm convinced that there are some amazingly talented, creative—and enthusiastic—grandparents hosting these camps, because I talked to a bunch of them! One grandma features a different craft each year that her grandchildren get to make during their special time together. Some grandparents I talked to have lake houses or a mountain retreat to host their Cousin Camp. Oh, how I'd love that! Another writes and directs a unique play each year that the grandkids perform the day their parents pick them up. But what really matters is the memories they make during the time spent together.

Sandy's Theater Camp 🍁

Sandy's theater camp evolved out of necessity. After a few days with all of her grandchildren together, they'd be at each other's throats and she'd be ready to pull her hair out. Some years she'd taken them to swimming lessons or Vacation Bible School during their week together, but the time came when they needed a new focus. She thought, *Well, I can't sing, but I could write a play for the grandkids to perform.* The first play she wrote was *The Mystery of the Diamond Ring.* When the grandkids arrived, they looked for costumes and props. Then came the week of rehearsals. On the last day, when their parents picked them up, they held the first performance. They had free time to swim and play, but not so much time to get on each other's nerves. Preparing and acting in the play was so much fun that they begged their grandma to write another one.

Next was *The Circus Play*; each child chose what performer he or she wanted to be. The local costume shop had just the right outfits for them to become Master of Ceremonies, Leo the

Lion, the Lion Tamer, the Strong Man, and circus clowns. Decked out in a flaming red wig, Grandma was the Master of Ceremonies' assistant. The Tightrope Walker balanced on a line of yellow tape on the carpet to the sound of the drum roll Grandpa provided from the computer. Three hula hoops provided the three rings and doubled as the rings the lion jumped through.

One of the children's favorite productions was *The Superhero Play*. Grandma acted out the girl who was kidnapped by the villain, Joker. The four younger children, on a mission to rescue her, chose to be Superman, Spiderman, Flash, and the Vulcan. A big part of the fun was picking out costumes and makeup. Each child received a copy of the script and added his or her own touches.

Sandy even edged in etiquette lessons at a friend's house one day. Before the play the grandchildren, dressed in black pants, white shirts, and bow ties, served their parents a proper three-course meal, which Sandy ordered from an Italian restaurant. With rehearsals, there was no time to cook. Then they changed into their costumes to perform as superheroes. Last year their play was *American Idol*, with Simon Cowell played by Grandpa, Paula Abdul played by Grandma, and host Ryan Seacrest played by the grandson who did not want to sing. The songs they performed ranged from the Mickey Mouse theme song to Elvis's *Hound Dog*; the kids came up with their own choreography. For the finale, all four sang *YMCA*, dressed as a policeman, a construction worker, a biker, and an Indian. Sandy's grandchildren are teenagers in high school now, and Adam, who was five when they started the theater camps, is now in middle school. They're working on their script for the next

> Early in the week, take a digital group picture of everyone wearing the same color T-shirt, or a shirt with your Cousin Camp logo and the date, which you can make with reverse transfers on white T-shirts. Let the cousins wear their camp T-shirts during the week, then take them home, along with a copy of the group photo.

play, and the photos and memories they've made working together will last far beyond the last performance.

Tips from the Experts for Smooth Sailing at Cousin Camp 🌿

Here are some helpful suggestions I gathered from the experts—the grandparents who have held cousin camps for 5 to 15 years.

Schedule the week well ahead of time. One grandparent I know sends a list of possible dates to each family and asks them to rate their top three choices, as well as nixing dates that won't work. It helps to do this early in the year or at Christmas, before other vacations are planned. Every year as the grandchildren get older and busier with their own activities, it's more challenging to set aside one week for Cousin Camp, but it can be done.

Start small. If you've never had a five- to seven-day camp for all your grandchildren (as I haven't since the great-aunts have hosted the cousin camps so far in our family), you might consider starting with a gathering of two to three days or a long weekend. Hosting a Cousin Sleepover or having two of the grandchildren at a time is a great way to start. This will leave the kids wanting more time together, and allow you to build up the program year after year.

Mary Jo Martin has grandchildren in Philadelphia, Denver, California, and Illinois. She prefers to have them come to Nana Camp two at a time; she does sewing projects with them and doesn't want them to have to wait too long for the sewing machine. In addition to their project of the week, they go to a nature center and museums, and spend lots of time playing in the tree house and exploring the trails and woods on the Martins' two-and-a-half acres.

Do what works for you. Marsha Van held "Honey Camp"—that's her grandma name—with all the grandchildren together, but it was so wild and crazy that she now hosts Honey Camp during five different weeks of the summer. Each grandchild gets his or her own week. They sing silly songs and play games She takes them to the YMCA to shoot baskets and ride the razor bikes. After work, GranDan takes the boys to hit golf balls.

Get organized and make a plan. Camp will be much more enjoyable if you've spent adequate time planning. Set aside a certain amount of money for activities and food. Let your grandchildren help plan activities and prepare meals. (See the sidebar on how to do this.) Be physically rested before they arrive and keep the week simple. Type up a medical permission form for each grandchild that gives you permission to authorize medical treatment in emergencies; be sure to include insurance information and both parents' signatures. For help in planning activities, seek out times to ask your grandchildren individually about what interests them. In doing this, a grandmother discovered that one of her grandchildren had always wanted a tree house. So the next summer they worked together to build one in the backyard. It was a huge success and they used it for many activities.

Get some help, and get grandpas involved. Having extra hands is particularly important if most of the grandchildren are close in age, or if there's a bunch of them and only one of you. Involve Grandpa and other family members whenever you can. For one Cousin Camp, a daughter and daughter-in-law kept up with the laundry and picked up toys at night. Barbara Erwin's husband was tired from working all day; she got him engaged in Cousin Camp by giving him a plan that eliminated surprises being sprung on him. He couldn't spend all day with the grandkids, but he was happy to take them putt-putt golfing and go-carting in the evenings.

At Cousin Camps, teen grandkids can take responsibility for helping with the younger children. Teenagers can help plan and lead games, assist in cooking, and be the older "buddy" for a younger cousin. If you have a devotional each day, let the teens read the story or use flannel board figures to illustrate a Bible story. If they play an instrument, encourage them to bring it and share their music with their cousins. If you have a flock of younger children, it helps to have one set of parents, an aunt, or your husband help you.

Delegate tasks. Then you'll have more energy to enjoy the fun activities you've planned. At Camp Ju-Ju, Grandpa is the activities director, Ju-Ju is spiritual director, and Great-Grandma heads up the kitchen and teaches a class on making pastries from scratch. Ann, the other grandma, is in charge of all the crafts.

Don't worry how the house looks—just for a week. It's amazing how fast children can mess up a home, but if we're constantly picking up, we may miss out on great moments together. If things are piling up, have a big 10- or 15-minute pick up before bed. The key is not to sweat the small stuff—so figure out before the grandkids arrive what's "small stuff" and what really matters.

Childproof your house. If you have young grandkids coming, put away cleaning fluids and medications, cover electrical outlets, and remove choking hazards from carpet and tables.

Choose some guidelines. A minimum number of "house rules" can help you have a more pleasant week together. Your boundaries will be different from other grandparents', depending on your home and the ages of the grandchildren. One grandma had fun rules like eating ice cream for breakfast and never making your bed. Another's included hopping five times when you enter the kitchen, and eating only in the kitchen or family room, not the living room. Another grandma made these boundaries: no running or roughhousing inside the house; take a bath or shower every night; and, get your own Popsicle out of the freezer whenever you'd like, but eat it in the garage or outside. You can even involve the older grandchildren in helping make house rules and writing them on poster board. Remember, setting house rules will help everyone have a great time.

Create a theme. Having a theme for the week gives you focus. It may be craft week, theatre week, or doing Vacation Bible School together with the grandteens serving as helpers. A group project creates harmony among the cousins—especially among all the boys! Last year the Poteets' Cousin Camp theme was "Love One Another"; this year it's "Fruit of the Spirit." Besides arts and crafts, they go swimming, boating, and fishing, and even feed the deer. This theme works wonderfully if you have a lake home.

The Hartsock grandchildren, who are between one and five years old, do simple activities that include playing with Play-Doh, finger-painting, blowing bubbles, swimming in a little pool on the deck, and a morning age-appropriate devotional. This year their theme is "Jesus first, others second, I'm third."

Peggy Powell started her Cousin Camp at her home in Texas by taking the grandkids on outings to the zoo and local parks. Now they gather in Colorado where the grandchildren rock climb, hike up Pikes Peak, and take trampoline or diving lessons together. A centerpiece activity this year will be finding 40 quarters the grandparents hide, and then brainstorming how they can invest money in someone who really needs help. When we do some creative planning…the possibilities are endless.

> I enjoyed spending time with the cousins and developing strong relationships during the week we spent each year at my grandma's. It was fun because we actually produced a play and yet we goofed off. I especially enjoyed all the laughter from the audience during the performances.
>
> —Wesley, age 15

You can make certain days special during Cousin Camp by designating a theme. On "Yellow Day" wear yellow clothing, eat yellow food, and take a walk around the neighborhood identifying things that are yellow. Next have "Backwards Day." Wear your clothes backwards and do things backward. Start your

Getting Grandpas Involved

There are plenty of ways for grandpas to be involved with grandchildren, not only during Cousin Camp, but at other times as well. Check out these ways that "Boomer" Powell interacted with his grandchildren gathered at his home this summer.

- He rode horses with all seven grandchildren on a mountain trail through beautiful forests. Boomer often takes the three grandsons to play golf while Grandma takes the granddaughters to tea at Glen Eyrie castle in Colorado Springs. He takes all of the grandchildren on golf cart rides, and they love it.

- One afternoon he laid his 6'1" body on the floor while the grandchildren used measuring tape to compare his height with Goliath's nine-foot frame.

- He told them stories of his expedition with 14 other men from the U.S. to look for Noah's ark in the mountains of Iran. Then he supervised the grandkids measuring the size of Noah's ark with four rolls of string on a football field.

- He knelt and prayed specifically for each grandchild, putting his hands on their shoulders and blessing them.

- He led the children in writing messages to our military troops to accompany the camouflage-covered Bibles their church is sending to combat zones.

"Patriotic Day" by singing "The Star Spangled Banner." Dress in red, white, and blue. Give everyone an American flag; decorate bikes, scooters, and tricycles, and have a parade around the neighborhood. On "Lemonade Stand Day," set up a lemonade stand in the front yard. With the profits, head for the discount store to buy a toy. What other inspirations for special days will pop from your imagination?

Granddad and the Measuring Stick

When our kids were young, we traveled to another state to visit their grandparents. As soon as we arrived, their granddad would have them stand beside the pantry door and mark their height on the door molding, along with their names and ages. Even when they were teens they loved seeing how much they had grown since the last visit. When Granddad moved and we gathered up his things, the treasured family record was pried off the door frame and went home with us. One Christmas after our children had families of their own, I bought long pieces of wooden door molding just like Granddad's, marked it in inches and feet, then used a special colored marker for each family member, marking their age and height through the years. Every grown child and grandchild was excited to receive the "Family History of Height." They're now using it to record their own children's heights.

—Carol Graves

Involve the grandchildren in preparing food for the week. "From the first I started a food scrapbook with pictures of child-friendly foods," said Deann Styles. The children go through the book and show her what they would like to have when they are in charge of a meal. Some of the top food choices are: breakfast tacos, cereal, sandwiches, pastas, pizza, hamburgers, hot dogs, lots of fruit, ice cream, crackers, Popsicles they make, and cookies they bake. They try to stick to simple, creative foods. Of course, there is always peanut butter and jelly. She assigns two children per meal to be helpers, and also assigns clean up crews. These duties are posted on the refrigerator as are the schedules and special activities for the day. Once or twice during the week they order take-out or coordinate a field trip with a meal at a restaurant.

Cousin Camp Closing

Plan a closing program for the last day of Cousin Camp. Invite each grandchild to share his or her favorite activities and stories of the week. Give each one a Cousin Camp T-shirt with the year on it. You may want to include another gift, such as a framed photo of the whole group of cousins with the grandparents. Close with a song or scavenger hunt.

Mary Jo, an Illinois grandma, has each child decorate a wooden photo frame made by Granddad. Each They paint the frame and add painted wooden letters that spell out, "Camp Nana, 200X." The frame holds a photo of the grandparents and the individual grandchild. This special gift goes home with each child.

> Cousin Camp is a time to get away from everyday life, think about things, and still have lots of fun.
> —Brian, 12

Consider celebrating the week with a photo book for each child. Pictures taken during the week will help grandkids hold those memories close as they head for their homes around the country.

Veteran Cousin Camp directors—loving grandparents I've talked to—remind us that it's important to focus on the grandkids rather than worrying about making each activity perfect or sticking to an exact agenda. Spend time individually with each child. Establish traditions, such as making a Cousin Camp shirt. And be sure to give the grandchildren an opportunity to reflect on their favorite times during the week before they go home. This will lock these special times in their memories and build excitement for what is to come in the years ahead.

> ### For the yearly Cousin Camp,
> we designed a grandchildren's dorm in the lower level of our house: a pink room for the girls and khaki room for the boys, with bunk beds and their own bath. I collected American Girl dolls and clothes for the girls, and PaPaw Bill built a huge Brio train table out of birch plywood. Each year he has a wood project they can work on in the garage with close supervision. Ping Pong, shooting baskets, taking walks to a pond to observe the swans and geese, swimming at the neighbor's pool every day, trips to baseball games and museums, family movies with popcorn, a daily Bible time from PaPaw with artistic visuals to support the lesson, lots of laughter, hugs, and love—memories which last a lifetime. We hold hands and pray at every meal. Some evenings we make an outdoor fire in the chiminea and make s'mores and chase fireflies. Even though my grandchildren don't live as close as I'd love to have them live, I am still active in their lives and feel their love deeply. As I quilt or knit, I am praying for and remembering these special blessings God has given me.
>
> —Sue Punkay

Younger Grandchildren

If your grandchildren are too young for a Cousin Camp, you could have a Cousin Day. Kathy Bruce and her husband, Jim, of Mequon, Wisconsin, take four of their grandchildren to see Santa each year. They pick the grandkids up, take them to dinner, have their picture taken with Santa, then drop them back at their homes. Everyone has a great time and looks forward to carrying on the tradition.

What matters isn't how long your time together is or what you do, but the fun of being together and connecting heart to heart with cousins and grandparents.

Chapter 6

Traveling with Your Grandkids

If I knew it was going to be
this much fun,
I would have become a
grandparent first.

—Unknown

Linda Carlson found being a long-distance grandma challenging, especially when her 14 grandchildren were scattered in four different states. When marital and legal problems due to divorce complicated relationships, one set of grandchildren was restricted from traveling out of their home state. As years went by, Linda worried that the grandkids would soon be grown and wouldn't even remember each other. She started thinking how great it would be to get all the cousins together in one place, and let them experience flying, since most of them hadn't ever been on a plane.

At a concert, Linda was inspired by the song "If You're Gonna Dream, Dream Big." It was as if God were saying, "Go for it! I'll take care of the details." Then the wheels started turning. Linda soon chose the destination: Hot Springs, Arkansas. She began checking airfares and saving every dollar she could for this dream get-together. Then came 9/11 and heightened security worries; she wondered if she should risk taking the grandkids on an airplane at all. But God kept reassuring her—

and the cost of airfares dropped dramatically.

Because the dates they'd selected were after the racing season in Hot Springs, they were able to reserve some old but well-
kept and affordable cabins right on Lake Hamilton. Little by little all the plans fell into place, and finally the big day came.

Linda and three of the grandkids flew to Memphis. There
they met two others who flew in from Indianapolis. Five other
grandkids arrived from Tampa, Florida. After they boarded the
plane for Little Rock, the announcement came of a half-hour
delay. The flight attendant let the kids go two-by-two into the
cockpit and meet the pilots. All of a sudden, Linda heard seven-
year-old Laura's sweet little voice over the intercom saying, "Hi,
Grandma!"

> Grandchildren are treasures
> that can't be measured in
> dollars and cents.
> —Audrey Sherins

Linda's sister met them at the
Little Rock airport with her SUV
and a rental van. They piled in all
the grandkids and suitcases and headed for Hot Springs. Two
more grandchildren who lived nearby were driven by their parents. The others thought it was cool to travel with "just
Grandma" and no parents.

Their weekend reunion was packed with simple fun:
exploring Mountain Tower and the creek at Gulfa Gorge camp-
ground, seeing azaleas and dogwoods in the height of their glory
along the Promenade, playing Bingo, swimming and fishing in
the lake—and most of all, just being with the cousins and their
grandma. The 12 cousins, ages 5 to 15, did hands-on experi-
ments at a science museum. They loved the picnics Grandma
prepared because they got to catch up with each other as they
enjoyed their favorite summer foods.

When Linda returned home, she thanked God for giving
her the vision and provision to enjoy such a big dream trip with
her grandchildren and allowing the cousins to reconnect.

Different Trips for Different Grands

Connecting is what taking trips together is all about. With families spread across the country, grandparents can create a special bond when they embark on a journey with their grandkids. Getting away from home, exploring a new area, and eating out or over a campfire all provide great opportunities for building relationships.

Perhaps connecting with your grandkids through crafts or making pizzas and cookies isn't your style. You'd rather hit the road and have some concentrated time hiking in the Rocky Mountains, canoeing on a river, or spending a few nights in a lovely hotel with your pre-teen granddaughter, who of course, will want to shop.

An amazing number of grandparents take their grandchildren along on vacations. Travel agents say that intergenerational travel is the hottest trend. Though it may sound daunting to you to take a pre-teen or a teenager on a one- or two-week trip, there are plenty of grandparents who have paved the way for us. I've learned so much from them about taking creative trips geared to an individual grandchild. Look with me at some of the different ways grandparents are connecting with their grandkids "on the road."

Grand Travel Testimonies

The Stricklands, a Texas couple, take each grandchild on a special trip the year he or she turns 12. Their first granddaughter hit that milestone last April; they left for Cancun to spend a week snorkeling, zip-lining, swimming with dolphins, and horseback riding at an all-inclusive hotel. What adventurous grandparents they are! Frances also surprised her granddaughter with some "girl time" and a manicure at the hotel salon.

Every summer, the O'Hare family of Oklahoma City, and their grown children, their spouses, and all their grandchildren, go to Horn Creek, a family ranch in Colorado. There they can spend individual time with different grandkids on hikes and during evening game times. They explore the surrounding area and have lots of together time with both the kids and adults. The plus of holding this event at Horn Creek? The camp takes care of the meals.

Pam Egan, who lives in Santa Fe, New Mexico, has five grandchildren—three of them teens. When grandchildren turn "double digit," or 10 years old, Pam takes them anywhere in the world they would like to go. As Pam says, younger than 10 is too much responsibility for an overseas trip! When I heard about this "anywhere" trip, I thought, "What lucky grandkids!"

> **My summer trips with my grandparents** allowed me to spend time with an older generation and see different perspectives and experiences. I could see up close how my grandparents lived out their faith. I enjoyed fishing side by side with a man I loved and respected. I wanted to be just like him, and I cherish the memories that have stayed with me long after my grandparents have gone on to be with the Lord.
>
> —George, age 40

One of the boys asked to go to London and Paris, and Grandma was game for that. Her secret is that she always puts her young traveling companion in charge of a number of things on the trip. "That way they learn more and feel very grown up," Pam says. An added benefit is they really get to know the city they're visiting. For example, on the Paris and London trip, her grandson held the taxi money and the snack money. He read all the maps, told the taxi driver where they needed to go, and figured out tips. He read the menus and ordered for both of them, and also got to decide what time they got up, what time to eat, what he would wear each day, and what photos to take—nearly all the decisions.

A granddad who was in the U.S. State Department and served around the world in embassies from Norway to Cyprus and Russia (and fortunately had a sister who worked for Delta and shared free tickets), flew one of his teen grandkids each year to spend two weeks with him. Although he lived overseas most of their growing-up years, spending two weeks with their grandfather sightseeing, riding trains, perusing museums, monuments, and ruins, plus enjoying local food and markets was a bonding experience these teens never forgot.

The Stanleys of Colorado take each of their 11 grandchildren on an individual trip when they are eight years old. The trip might last from two to three days, depending on their destination. Because each of the 11 grandchildren is unique, they try to find a trip that would be interesting to each boy and girl. They talk about where to go and plan the trips a year or more ahead. The grandparents throw out suggestions and then add the element of surprise after deciding on the place. On the Christmas before the trip, they put a clue inside a small gift so the grandchild can guess where he or she gets to go on the special trip. Revealing the destination in this way has proved to be a hit.

One of the granddaughters asked to go to Chicago. They spent one night in a hotel, but packed in a lot of fun in the two days. They took her to the Aquarium, Navy Pier, and Rain Forest Café. They rode a Ferris wheel, saw an American Girl performance, and went to the American Girl café for lunch. Along the way they had some great conversations and a morning devotional together. One of the girls chose Williamsburg, Virginia. She loved all the historical sightseeing, the maze behind the governor's mansion, and especially the homemade gingerbread cookies and lemonade served under an old oak tree.

When grandson Matthew was eight, he wanted to go to a ranch. His granddad located a ranch and took Matthew on a two-and-a-half-day outdoor adventure with activities such as riding horses, hiking, and skeet shooting. One grandson opted to go to Mt. Rushmore. He loved everything about the trip: camping in a state park, going to the reptile museum, qualifying for his junior ranger badge, and sliding down a huge slide. Before they left Mt. Rushmore, Michael wanted to sit "just one more time" to look at the faces of Mt. Rushmore. It was such a meaningful time for him.

The Stanleys also took two of their granddaughters to Prince Edward Island. The girls had read *Anne of Green Gables* before the trip. They loved Avonlea—drinking raspberry cordial, dressing up in Avonlea costumes, giving hugs to Anne, Diana, and Prissy, and nostalgically reliving Anne's life.

I'm impressed by how creative grandparents can be in planning vacations to include grandkids. Beverly and George Hanson invite one of the grandchildren at a time to join them on their yearly Florida vacation. Taking the grandkids individually allows them one-on-one time with each child. With this approach there are no children's conflicts to resolve—not that their grandchildren ever argue! The three drive to Florida together, allowing ample car time for catching up.

When they arrive, they don't do a lot of costly activities. The grandchild gets to see relatives he or she only sees once a year, go sightseeing in Cortez—the town where their great-grandpa was born—enjoy the children's museum, and play on the beaches on the Gulf of Mexico. After two weeks, Anne's husband flies home with the grandchild. He stays home for a few weeks to take care of business, then flies back to Florida with another grandchild. After two weeks, the three fly home together. The Hansons love the special time with each grandchild; they pray about being a positive influence as the grandchildren get to know them better.

National Parks and Elderhostel Programs

With so many grandparents interested in taking the younger generation on trips, travel options have multiplied. There are camps that have all the activities of the week planned for you, pricey grandtravel cruises, and beach resorts that cater to kids and their grandparents.

In almost every state, national parks offer less expensive, equally memorable trips. Senior citizens, 62 and above, can get a lifetime pass to all national parks for only $10. Treasures like Yellowstone, the Great Smoky Mountains of Tennessee, Big Bend in Texas, and Glacier National Park in Montana provide inexpensive options for grandparents and grandkids who love to be in the great outdoors. Rangers lead an interesting variety of programs and activities for kids. Paved trails offer opportunities for fascinating hikes. To top it off, you'll find reasonable rates for cabins and lodges in the national parks.

Traveling with their grandparents, Hanni and Pops, has been a hit with my grandsons. They have loved their adventures to Hermit Basin, Silver Dollar City, and Horn Creek, and numerous camping and fishing trips to the lake.

One travel option I've discovered is the Intergenerational Elderhostel programs focused on exploring new subjects such as, "Migration Mysteries in Minnesota: Hawks on the Wing," "Wolves in the Wild," and "North Country Settlers." Other options include a tour of the Grand Canyon and a weeklong stained glass painting workshop. For many years, Elderhostel has been a great travel institution for seniors. Now it allows grandchildren to participate in over 300 of the travel adventures. Some of the Elderhostel weeks cost less than six hundred dollars for everything. Others cost more. They are held all over the country and overseas, as well as at college campuses, national parks, and historical sites.

> For a forest scavenger hunt in a national park or neighborhood nature area, search for acorns, bird nests, feathers, two types of ferns, three types of pine cones, differently shaped leaves, wildflowers, and two kinds of rocks.

A Texas grandma named Clara goes on Elderhostel trips and has taken many of her grandkids along—sometimes one grandchild at a time and sometimes two. Recently she returned from a marine life excursion trip on a boat out of Galveston,

Texas, with her 13-year-old grandson. Because he is interested in oceanography, the weekend was right up his alley.

Toledo, Ohio, grandparents Anne Basile and her husband, Robert, took their youngest grandson Eric on three different Elderhostel trips when he was 10 and 11 years old. They found there were numerous benefits to these trips: Interacting with their grandson without parents along and sharing the experiences of the week strengthened their relationships and forged new bonds. They came away with a better understanding of the other's generation, having had a chance to observe their grandchild with peers and learn from each other.

One of the trips was to the Kettunen Center in Michigan. It focused on rocketry, fish biology, casting, lake ecology, and bird-watching. The Elderhostel week in Kentucky was at Otter Creek State Park; Eric got to participate in archery, canoeing, hiking, rappelling, and spelunking. The next year was Aerospace week in Virginia. It included a field trip to Virginia Air and Space Center for hands-on activities, a tour of Langley Field, a Cessna flight, and the challenge of building an imaginary living station on Mars using throwaway materials. Seeing this child board a small Cessna airplane was a scary moment, but Anne wouldn't trade the exciting learning experiences they had together. One of the most memorable activities

Since I was so young

when I went to Elderhostels with my grandparents, I'm glad Grandma made scrapbooks to help me remember. Seeing the pictures and hearing her talk about them makes me realize she and Grandpa enjoyed them almost as much as I did. I'm so grateful to my grandparents for taking such great interest and care in my life.

—Eric Notziger, now 21

for Eric was building a 15-inch rocket and launching it himself. What a fortunate young man! (If you're interested in receiving an Elderhostel catalog, call 877-426-8056.)

Preparing for Grandtravel ✼

These adventuresome grandparents have found that planning for the big trip is important to the success of the journey. Think about these things as you prepare.

Find out what activities are available that you and your grandchild could both enjoy.

Make sure your grandchild has opportunities to exercise and get the wiggles out. Keep the child's interests in mind. A child who is afraid of water might not have a great time at the beach. But that same child might love a dude ranch, if she likes riding horses.

Once you've decided on the destination, aim for a balance between things you enjoy and things your grandchild would choose. Let your grandchild help you with the planning. This is especially important for pre-teens and teenagers. Encourage them to choose daily activities. Making these choices gives them ownership of the trip and keeps them engaged.

Make a budget for the transportation, lodging, and activities you're planning; don't forget to include daily spending money for each grandchild. Even if it's a small amount for souvenirs or candy, if you give it to them each day instead of all at once, they'll be happier travelers.

Be realistic about your own energy level and your grandchild's limitations. Kids are like Energizer bunnies that keep going and going and going, even when you'd like to take a nap. Does your grandson have the attention span for a three-hour tour of a historic naval ship? Is the grandchild old enough to be without her parents and not be fraught with nightmares?

If in doubt, try an overnight at your house first, then maybe a short weekend outing. As you plan, talk with the parents about your ideas, the child's maturity, and the various parts of the trip. Consult them often; they know their kids best.

I hope to take each of my grandsons, who are now five, six, and seven, on the Heartland Flyer, an Amtrak train that runs from Oklahoma City to Ft. Worth, Texas. They'll be able to enjoy a day at the Ft. Worth Stockyards, better known to them as "Cowboy Town." That will be a good start for our travel adventures.

Build excitement and interest by showing grandkids travel books and maps of where you're going. Check your library for books or videos about your destination. If you live a long distance from your grandchild, share photos via e-mail or send her a travel book of the special places you're going to visit.

Share with your grandkids your guidelines and expectations for their behavior in public places such as hotels, restaurants, and museums.

Better safe than sorry is a good guideline when traveling with our grandchildren. We hope they don't hurt themselves or get sick, but we need to be prepared just in case. Make up a first-aid kit containing essentials such as antibiotic ointment, Band-Aids, chewable Pepto-Bismol, acetaminophen, cream for bug bites, sunscreen, and cold medicine approved by their parents. Make sure you have the mom and dad sign a medical permission form, handwritten or typed, that authorizes you to make decisions in case of an emergency. Have a copy of each child's birth certificate. Give parents copies of your reservations and itinerary. Have a plan in place ahead of time for what you will do if the child gets lost—heaven forbid!

By the Sea, By the Sea

If you go to the shore, a seaside scavenger hunt is a great way to whet your grandchild's appetite for science and oceanography and sharpen his observation skills. Most of all, it's a wonderful way to have a good time together.

Try these hunting tips:

- Pair older members of the family with younger ones.
- Wear rubber boots or tennis shoes.
- The best time to find sea creatures is at low tide.
- Hand out a list of sea animals with a challenge to find as many as they can.
- Draw pictures for pre-readers, or let their team members guide them in looking for hermit crabs, attached barnacles, different types of shells, sea grasses, fiddler crabs, sea urchins, starfish, lobster parts, snails, sand dollars, gulf feathers, and driftwood.
- Just for fun, hide a piece of "golden treasure"—a shiny coin—in the sand.

More Tips for Traveling with Grandchildren

For a grandchild, a journey with grandparents, whether a week, a weekend, or a one-day outing to a fun destination, can become a special memory. Paying attention to details will help make the journey a pleasant one.

Don't be in a hurry. One of the things grandkids love about traveling with grandparents is that Grandma and Grandpa aren't as rushed as their parents. If the grandchild wants to stop and swing on a tree, let her do it. Avoid having such a packed agenda that you are rushing the children around from activity to activity without time to chill out and enjoy things. That's what many kids do year-round; it wouldn't feel like a vacation! Let them pause to examine a spider creeping along a stone wall. Be open to moments of serendipity. Keep it simple and don't overbook the trip. The best memories are made when you go at a pace you both enjoy.

Make the trip age-appropriate. When Mom and Dad Gardners' granddaughters turned four years old, they took each one individually for a day outing to the American Girl Doll museum. Apparently, that's a very favorite place for little girls! They enjoyed teatime at the bistro, and got to pick out their birthday presents. They listened to the American Girl books and music on the way up and enjoyed one-on-one time with Grandma. When they are seven, the girls will go back again, this time to see the American Girl Doll Show.

The Gardners' first grandson will turn four in 2009. Grandpa has a trip lined up to take him to the Lego Store and the Hershey Factory. Maybe they'll even explore the ESPN Zone and the Harley-Davidson store.

As children get older, they can handle a weekend trip, then a week away from home with grandparents. Each child is an individual; their maturity levels vary widely. At eight or nine, some aren't yet ready to spend the night away from their parents, even with a favorite friend. So if you're planning to take them on a week long journey, take a trial run! Months before a long trip, start small by taking a day trip to the zoo or another kid-friendly site. Short trips can also help you find out what kinds of activities they like best.

If you take more than one grandchild on a trip, have them wear matching T-shirts or baseball caps. Announce, "Today's yellow! Everybody wear yellow today!" This helps tremendously when you're trying to keep track of them in a crowd.

Practical clothes for travel include a many-pocketed vest for when you are in public with the grandchildren. Peggy, who has taken several grandkids at a time on an outing, tells me that this equips you to wear everything you need, without the hassles of a purse. At times you'll find that you need both your hands free. Peggy has also learned from experience that you should make sure your grandkids know your cell phone number, especially when you go to an amusement park, public park, or any busy place where children may get distracted and wander. Write your cell number on masking tape, then stick it to their shirts on the inside, near the hem. This makes it handy for grandkids to give your phone number to a security officer or park official.

> **When our grandson John was three,** we took his family to Mexico for a vacation after Christmas. We stayed at a place that had a wonderful breakfast buffet every morning. John was in a phase of not eating very well. One morning my husband brought back a huge plate of pancakes smothered in Nutella, that yummy hazelnut chocolate spread, to see if John would eat that. John hesitated but then took a bite, closed his eyes, looked up to heaven and said, "Ohhhhh, Papa, I have been dreaming of this my whole life!"
>
> —Jane Robinson

Take some travel snacks based on the grandchildren's preferences. Sometimes you may go miles between meals, and they'll be happier campers if their tummies aren't empty. Small packages of peanut butter crackers (if they're not allergic to peanuts), cheese sticks, fruit roll-ups, individual cereal boxes, individual packs of cookies or chips, and water bottles are great to keep on hand. Make sure the snacks aren't all sugar-laden or you'll have the grandkids bouncing off the walls. Check with the grandchild who's going on the trip—and his or her parents—to see what he or she prefers for snacks.

Encourage the child to bring his or her own backpack and to carry a favorite stuffed animal, toy, book, or game. These familiar things will definitely come in handy on the journey.

Sample Medical Authorization

Here is a very simple example of the kind of form you'll need in case a medical emergency arises while your grandkids are in your care.

We give _____

(grandparent names)

authority to obtain any medical procedures or medication necessary for our children,

_____

_____

(names of children)

Signed: _____ and

_____, Parents

A parent's cell phone number:

_____

Date _____

Remember, no matter how well you prepare, life happens, especially when traveling with kids. Unexpected setbacks such as motion sickness, traffic jams, rain, bad moods, and lost luggage can cause glitches in our plans. But if you have some "Plan B" ideas in case things go awry and are armed with a good sense of humor, flexibility, and a lollipop or candy bar, you can still enjoy the time together. And perhaps you'll even create a happy memory you never planned.

Good Things to Take When You're Traveling with Kids

* nightlight
* first aid kit
* small bottle of antibacterial hand gel
* sunscreen
* zip-top bags
* camera, plus a disposable camera for the grandchild
* cap or visor for each person
* Frisbee or small foam football for exercise break (especially if you're traveling in a car)
* deck of cards and small travel games
* paper and colored pencils

Traveling through Life Together

Once I met a grandma and granddaughter who'd just enjoyed a seven-day coach tour through England and Scotland for an eighth-grade graduation gift. The grandmother wasn't a woman of means; she'd saved for many months to take her granddaughter on a special trip. As they told me about their adventures exploring Shakespeare's house and seeing real bag-pipers on a corner in Edinburgh playing "Amazing Grace," their eyes lit up with memories. And I sensed that it was all worth it to share those experiences together.

You don't have to be wealthy to take a memory-making trip with your grandchild. I've talked to grandkids whose travel experiences with grandparents meant going to a lake house 50 miles away or simply having a blast in their grandparents' back-yard. I was touched by the joy of a little girl who loved having her first hotel experience with Grandma; she especially enjoyed the swimming pool and the nice restaurant.

> **The bridges that grandparents build last for generations.**
> —Anonymous

The plans and destination don't matter so much—what matters is that Grandma and Grandpa care enough to be involved in the life of their grandchild and take the time to get to know each other better. One grandma sets aside money from her part-time home business for adventure trips with the grandkids. Others save a portion of their income each month for a special outing or overnight. All of us can save money by going off-season, using senior discounts, and checking out budget travel Web sites. It takes some planning, effort, and funds, but the bond we form with our grandchildren and the memories we make "on the road" are a great investment.

Chapter 7

Visiting—At Your House and Theirs

*You never know when
you're making a memory.*
—Ricky Lee Jones

Sitting on top of Carol's microwave in the kitchen is a heart-shaped red velvet box with a special treasure inside. The box originally came as a valentine gift with candy inside, but she filled it with buttons collected over the years to entertain her grandchildren.

One day she thought it might be fun to sit down with her granddaughter and look at all the buttons. As they sorted through the collection, they found all kinds of interesting ways to group the buttons: by size, by color, and by shape. They sorted the buttons to see which colors were most and least common. They played "Find the Button," as Carol described a specific button and her granddaughter searched for it. When they get together, her granddaughter likes to find her favorite pearl, silver, and gold buttons and imagine who would wear such finery. Carol hopes her granddaughter will always remember their time together when she sees that velvet heart box filled with buttons.

When our grandchildren visit our house, we don't spend a fortune entertaining them. We play board and card games, take them to the local library to check out books to read together, or make cookies. We sometimes throw a ball or Frisbee around in the backyard and visit a kids' museum. Most of all, we let them chill out. Most children and teens today are so busy and their parents lead such hectic lives that they don't have much time to just be.

Spending Individual Time with Each Grandchild 🍁

One of the keys to connecting with our grandchildren is finding ways to spend one-on-one time with them during visits at their house or ours. Maybe we can't do it very often, but even once or twice a year makes a difference. A friend of mine takes her grandson and two of his best friends on a day outing once a year. She picks a place they'd be interested in, such as the fire station or military museum. Then she takes them out for a special meal and they spend the night. That way she gets to know both her grandson and his friends better.

> **When we were with**
> our three-year-old granddaughter, she had to go to the hospital for stitches above her eyebrow. The nurse asked for Sophie to follow her fingers with her eyes. I'm sure Sophie lost interest in this rather quickly, so the nurse said, "Sophie, where are my fingers?"
> Sophie proudly and promptly responded, "In your glove!"
> —Kathy Bruce

When I visit Milwaukee where our son Chris and his wife Maggie live with their two little girls, I've established a tradition of taking six-year-old Josephine to Denny's for breakfast—just the two of us. The first time we went, she'd only seen the advertising billboards along the road and thought it must be a grand restaurant. It became "our place." From the green powder that made her water green and fizzy to the pancakes piled high with strawberries, this outing was a hit. Spending time alone gave us a chance to talk about Josephine's favorite things about school and how she liked her Daisy (pre-Brownie Scout) group and swimming lessons. I look forward to taking her little sister Lucy on a breakfast outing when she's old enough.

Another grandma has a "Starbucks outing" whenever she travels to California to visit her 11-year-old granddaughter. The two walk to the coffee shop where Ashlyn feels like a big girl ordering a decaf cappuccino and a pastry treat. As they talk and catch up, her grandmother listens and focuses her full attention on what Ashlyn is saying. Although it's a short, simple activity, they both savor the moments together.

When we spend one-on-one time with a grandchild, we fill her emotional tank without the distractions of other siblings vying for attention. That child feels special that Grandma or Grandpa made time to spend individually with her. So that the other grandkids don't feel left out, we need to schedule time with each of the siblings. It may be short, but making a date for an individual outing, even if it's just taking a walk together, builds your relationship. You can start with making a trip to the local playground and buying a snow cone afterward. Then try an afternoon or a full-day trip to a children's museum and have lunch together. The most important thing is to give each grandchild some extra-special attention. One of the best ways to do that is to listen to them.

Emotionally Connecting with Our Grandkids: The Value of Listening

When we're with our grandchildren, whether at their house or ours, it's easy to be preoccupied with checking e-mail, straightening the house, preparing the next meal, or talking to a friend on the phone. But making the most of a visit means taking time to listen to our grandchildren, being emotionally available, and learning about them. It's one of the greatest gifts we can give them and the number one relationship-builder.

More than anything else, young people long to be listened to. They want to feel accepted, understood, and valued by us. Listening well fills all three of these needs. It's one of the most important ways we can connect and build a relationship. Try these suggestions to improve your listening skills.

When your grandchild is talking or requests your attention, give her eye contact and pay attention to her words, feelings, and body language. Though you may be tempted to offer your opinions or advice, effective listening builds a much closer connection. For teenagers, it's the top way for grandparents to show their love and support. We can let them know that we're open to hearing them express both positive and negative feelings.

> ### I started a tradition
> with my grandson as soon as he began eating grown-up food. Since I live out of town, soon after arriving, I take him to IHOP and we have pancakes. We talk and eat and often go to the zoo or a movie afterward, spending two to four hours together—just the two of us. He looks forward all year to this special time with his grandma.
>
> —Barbara Wade

Start small. Instead of aiming to listen for an hour, start with a goal of spending five or ten minutes a day tuning in to what your grandchild is saying. Do something that promotes conversation, like taking a destination walk or a drive together, stopping for a slushy, or a having a hot chocolate if it's winter.

Be available to talk about sensitive subjects without overreacting. If you overreact to what your grandkids share—especially adolescents—they tend to clam up.

Ask good questions, the open-ended kind, not to interrogate but to understand where they're coming from. Closed questions can be answered with a yes or no and close the door on conversation. Open-ended questions such as, "What happened?" or "How do you feel about that?" encourage thinking and communication and don't have a right or wrong answer. You can also stimulate conversation with creative questions such as; "What would it be like to have wings instead of arms? What things could you do that you can't now?" If you sense that your grandchild doesn't want to talk, it's best not to push.

Practice active listening. Active listening doesn't judge the words that come out of a grandchild's mouth. Avoid saying, "Honey, you shouldn't feel like that," or, "It's not so bad; you'll get over it," if your grandson speaks angrily about not being chosen for a team. Instead, practice listening effectively by saying, "It sounds like you're mad and hurt about not being picked for the team. I can sure understand that!" Let a grandchild know he or she is really heard before offering solutions for a problem.

Avoid moralizing, criticizing, or saying, "That's not what we did in the old days." Those are communication-busters. So are changing the subject and interrupting while the child is talking.

Avoid criticizing their parents or disagreeing with parents' decisions. Remember, even though your visit may be focused on the grandchildren, your son, daughter, or daughter-in-law might love some attention and listening time as well. Affirming what a great job they are doing as parents provides much-needed support and makes for harmonious family relationships.

Grandparents: A Lifeline in Troubled Times

When we're sensitive to our grandchildren and available to listen, we can make a huge difference when they go through loss and struggles. Take, for example, Susan Douglass, who lives in England and has two grandsons ages four and twenty months. Their paternal grandma died tragically two years ago at the age of 56, so she only knew the older boy, James. "She was his

'Nana' and I am his 'Nanny,'" Susan told me. James had spent much time at Nana's house and they loved each other dearly. Young as he was, he liked to talk about his Nana.

Instead of changing the subject or thinking she had to distract him into play so he wouldn't be sad, Susan let him take the lead. When he wanted to, she helped him remember all the lovely things about Nana. As they read a book together, a picture might trigger him to chat about Nana. They looked at a photograph of her so he could see her smile. This was never morbid, but rather a warm sharing of someone who was so special to him. Though his memories may dim as the years pass, Susan always wants James to know that he had another Nana who loved him as much as she does.

We can ease the ache of loss as Susan did, and be a refuge for our grandchildren in good times and bad, just by listening and empathizing.

Grandma's House; Our Favorite Place

Last winter Donna Knip's daughter and son-in-law took their three little ones to Disneyland and Sea World. All three children said Sea World was the best place they'd ever been.

Joni, their mom, asked, "Better than Disney World?"

"Yes," they answered.

"Better than the zoo?" which is one of their favorite places.

"Yes, better than the zoo," they said in unison.

Joni named other places, and the kids' answer was always "Yes!"

Finally she asked, "Was it better than Grandma Non's?"

They looked at her, shocked she'd even asked, and said, "No! Grandma's house is the BEST!"

When Donna heard that if her grandchildren could choose to go anywhere, they would choose to come to her house, she pondered the reason. An e-mail her daughter Kristi sent soon afterward answered that question.

The kids enjoy playing blocks, cars, making towns in the play room, playing baseball, watching movies, and dressing up with Grandma's real shoes. But I really don't think those are the main things about why Grandma and Grandpa's house is so special to them. Your house is the epitome of comfort for them. They always feel welcome and at home. They feel loved and accepted. Why? Because of Grandma and Grandpa! You make them feel valuable and worthy. You listen to their stories and happenings and all-important opinions. You cuddle them when there are hurt feelings among the cousins or if a wall jumps out and bumps someone. You make time for lunch with them and prepare meals with foods you know each one will enjoy. You have drawers and cabinets filled with candy and child-size cups, and baskets with paper and markers. And most of all, you love each one for who they are and how God made each one different and special. Thanks, Mom!

The Cookie Press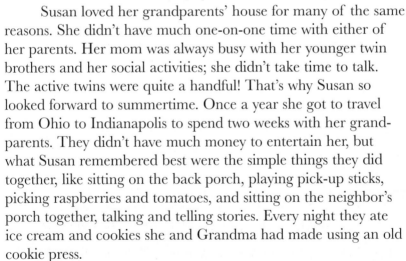

Susan loved her grandparents' house for many of the same reasons. She didn't have much one-on-one time with either of her parents. Her mom was always busy with her younger twin brothers and her social activities; she didn't take time to talk. The active twins were quite a handful! That's why Susan so looked forward to summertime. Once a year she got to travel from Ohio to Indianapolis to spend two weeks with her grandparents. They didn't have much money to entertain her, but what Susan remembered best were the simple things they did together, like sitting on the back porch, playing pick-up sticks, picking raspberries and tomatoes, and sitting on the neighbor's porch together, talking and telling stories. Every night they ate ice cream and cookies she and Grandma had made using an old cookie press.

If the State Fair was going on, the three of them went together. One warm evening they took Susan to the little amusement park in town. When Grandpa came home from work each day, Susan would hide and Grandpa would find her. Grandma put her old costume jewelry in a trinket box and let Susan wear it.

Even though Susan's grandparents weren't close in proximity, they were very close to her heart. During phone calls and short visits they gave her something she received from no one else in her life. When she was with them, she was the most wonderful and special person. Susan doesn't remember one toy they ever gave her. It was just the simple things—their love and the time they spent with her—that filled a huge place in her heart and life.

> The presence of grandparents in children's lives has a reassuring effect; they provide stability, continuity, and hopefully, role models for parenting,
> happiness, and success.
> —Archie Dunham

The summer visits lasted until Susan was 15, but the heart-to-heart connection lasted her whole life. When her grandma died, Susan got to keep the beloved cookie press. She uses it in her own kitchen today to make cookies for her sons and grandsons.

Helping Grandkids Feel at Home

Setting aside a place for toys on our glass-walled sun porch lets my grandchildren know that they are welcome and that they have a special place here. Their corner is stocked with a dollhouse, a craft table, building blocks, and a big basket filled with costumes, plastic army men, cars, and toys. One grandma I know keeps a dresser with a drawer labeled for each of her five grandchildren. When they visit, they not only put their clothes in the drawer, but check it for a new book or pair of shorts.

Other simple things that say "Welcome!" include:

✳ A toothbrush for each grandchild with his or her name on it. Now there are musical toothbrushes and superhero or princess toothbrushes, so pick a favorite!

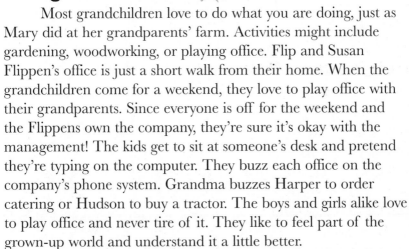

❋ A stepstool in the bathroom so they can reach the sink by themselves, and perhaps their own towel

❋ A bookshelf with "can't miss" children's stories

❋ A toy box or big drawer with puzzles, stuffed animals, games, dolls, and musical toys

❋ A highchair and portable crib (easy to find and inexpensive at garage sales) for the little ones, sippy cups, booster chairs, and a car seat

❋ A night-light in the bedroom, a gate if you have a flight of stairs, and safety features that child-proof your home

❋ A place for teen grandkids to charge their cell phones and iPods and connect to the Internet

Doing What You Do

Most grandchildren love to do what you are doing, just as Mary did at her grandparents' farm. Activities might include gardening, woodworking, or playing office. Flip and Susan Flippen's office is just a short walk from their home. When the grandchildren come for a weekend, they love to play office with their grandparents. Since everyone is off for the weekend and the Flippens own the company, they're sure it's okay with the management! The kids get to sit at someone's desk and pretend they're typing on the computer. They buzz each office on the company's phone system. Grandma buzzes Harper to order catering or Hudson to buy a tractor. The boys and girls alike love to play office and never tire of it. They like to feel part of the grown-up world and understand it a little better.

One weekend when Jessica and Christopher were visiting, they left with Papaw for a while. Susan, their grandma, assumed they were going on one of their long walks as Papaw loves nature and that's something he and the grandkids do together. A couple of hours later the kids came running up to the house with smiles on their faces. She asked, "Where have you been?"

Christopher responded with a big smile, "We've been playing office with Papaw." Susan had difficulty imagining such a thing. A successful entrepreneur for both business and social causes, Papaw always moved at a fast pace. He was not one to sit still at a computer.

Then little Jessica explained, "Yeah, we were buying and sellin' companies!" She laughed at the contrast of her way of playing office and Papaw's version of the same game. As Susan says, "The kids loved them both, which shows they are capable of anything. There is so much potential in them to sell tractors, be a mommy, and even buy and sell companies. And we as grandparents get the privilege of helping them discover their gifts and find what it is they were created to do."

If you have a home office, you can stock it with an old phone, office supplies, lots of paper, and an invoice book. Or, when grandkids visit, take them to work with you for a morning and lunch out at a restaurant. You never know—you may be the catalyst for one of your grandchildren to become a successful businessperson!

Things to Remember When Visiting at Their House

You've set aside time to take a grandparent trip, packed everything, including a few surprises and gifts, and endured the hassles of flying across the country. You're anticipating a lovely trip filled with lots of connecting time. But soon after your arrival, you can tell that your daughter-in-law is irritated by something you said. Later that evening, she criticizes you for rocking the baby too long and not staying on their schedule. When you pick up all the toys and clothes on the floor, she feels you're looking down on her housekeeping and gets her feelings hurt. Your spirits flag as you realize you will be there for five more days, and you wonder how you can make the most of your time without making somebody mad or taking things personally.

Trips to the grandkids' houses can be a blessing—both to them and to us—and that's what we hope for. But since we're all human and prone to mistakes, it's easy to fall into miscommunication or thoughtlessness and make the visit go awry.

I've learned so much both from trial and error on my own grandma visits, and also from wise grandparents I interviewed on this issue. Here are some tips that may contribute to a harmonious visit on your grandkids' turf.

> ### I loved going to visit my grandparents
> on their farm in Texas when I was a child. From the time we arrived I would follow my grandfather around like a shadow. He would take me with him to do the chores: milk the cow, gather eggs from the chicken coop, and walk the fields checking on the crops. I still remember the first time he showed me how to milk a cow. That was fine, but no way was this "city girl" going to drink the milk we gathered in the pail from the cow! So, "Pa" would drive many miles into the nearest town and buy me "homogenized" milk to drink. I'd help my grandmother shell peas or peel pears for her pear jam. My favorite time was after dinner when I would sit in a rocking chair with them on their screened-in porch and Pa would sing me, "You Are My Sunshine." Fifty years later I sing that same song to our grandsons...and still miss my grandfather.
>
> —Mary Mayer

Instead of rushing in to do a project you think will benefit their home or family, ask your grown son, daughter, or daughter-in-law whether they'd like you to do it. Don't assume you know what their major needs are. Maybe they'd rather you sit on the floor and play with the grandchildren instead of painting the kitchen. Asking, "How can I help you today or this week?" can make the visit a success. While you're there, go to bed early and read after the grandchildren are asleep so the parents have time to connect and be alone. Giving them some space makes for a more pleasant visit for all.

Be willing to go with how they discipline their children. One set of grandparents is so afraid they'll do it wrong when they travel from Michigan to Oregon for a visit at their son and daughter-in-law's house that they avoid being alone with the grandchildren at all. If you're in doubt about what to do about bedtime, tantrums, or time-out, ask the parents and respect their ways of doing things. If they are trying to feed the children a healthy diet and keep sweets to a minimum, follow their lead.

Memories Are Made of This
When you have been at your grandchild's house for a visit and it's time to go home, leave something behind so that sweet memories will remain. It might be a love note hidden under her pillow, a box of homemade brownies in the kitchen, a framed photo of the two of you beside her bed, or clues that lead to a treat. Whatever thoughtful thing you leave, it will be appreciated and remind your grandchild that though you're gone, you're thinking of her.

Be financially sensitive. One grandma I know realizes that her daughter and son-in-law who live in another country are on a tight budget. So when she spends two weeks at their home, she buys a week of groceries at the local market and includes a special treat they can't afford, like real orange juice or a favorite ice cream. She offers to make dinner and takes the family out to eat to give Mom a much-needed night off.

When they visit in the Middle Eastern country where their

adult children and grandchildren serve on the mission field, some long-distance grandparents I know invite the whole team of missionaries to their hotel and host a swimming party and cookout. Since the other missionaries are just like family to their kids, this is a double blessing. They get to know those people who are closest to their family and they give the whole group a memorable evening.

Remember that each daughter or daughter-in-law and son or son-in-law is unique and has different needs. What they most need might be a morning or two to sleep in while you feed the grandchildren breakfast or take them out for doughnuts (and bring some back for the parents). One daughter-in-law might appreciate a date night out because they can't afford a babysitter. Babysitting while the parents are out gives you special time to know your grandchildren. Be sensitive and ask what the parents would most appreciate when you visit their house.

> ### We live in Fairfax, Virginia;
> our grandchildren, Emma and Anna Maria, live in Japan. When we visit them once a year we spend a lot of time doing things they like. For example, Anna Maria loves games so almost every day we play games. Also, Abo (their grandpa) likes to do magic tricks. This is big with Anna Maria! She likes to try and figure out how he does his tricks. "Magic Night" is fun for all of us. Also, we try to let Cristina and Jason go out for dinner or the movies while we keep the girls, and they love it. The last time we went to Hawaii when they were stationed there, we sent them off on a three-day trip to one of the other islands; it was great for them. It is a little bit difficult being so far away, but we make the most of our visits and keep in touch daily throughout the year.
> —Maria Cayere

Go with an attitude of "How can I serve?" instead of expecting your family to serve you. It's hard to take care of three little kids all day with no respite, especially when you have company. Today's parents are very stressed; offering to help gives them support. If you pitch in with your daughter-in-law's duties around the house, after asking if she'd like your help, then your son or daughter and their spouses will have more time to play and visit. Avoid spending your time reorganizing a cluttered room or making suggestions about how the house could be cleaner—it's intimidating to young parents. People who live with little children rarely have perfect houses—and anyway, people are more important than housekeeping perfection. Pray before you go that God will make you a blessing, not only to your grandchildren, but to their parents as well.

Connect with your grandchild's school and teacher. During the week you are visiting, make it a point to visit your grandchild's school by picking her up and meeting the teacher. Or you could schedule your trip to fall on Grandparents Day when grandmoms and granddads are invited into the classroom. When our son and daughter-in-law lived in St. Louis, my husband and I scheduled a trip there so we could attend the Grandparents' Tea hosted by our granddaughter Caitlin's third-grade class. They showed their art, performed a play, gave each grandparent a gift they had made, and held a lovely teatime with cookies. We were the only grandparents from out of state, and how we enjoyed this time! It was such a treat to be there and meet our grandson Caleb's friends and his kindergarten teacher, and to see the classroom where he learned each day and the playground where he played.

"We attend Grandparents Day faithfully," said Jan Pieper, a Houston grandmother of four. "It is actually a highlight in our lives each year. It happens in November, right before the break for Thanksgiving. Our grandkids in Dallas know it would take an act of Congress to make us miss that very special event. Going to Grandparents Day is very important to us because it sets the tone for our holiday season. It puts things in proper perspective, having given thanks together for the importance of family down through the generations." During basketball and soccer season, they also try to attend a game for each of the grandchildren.

30 Kisses

A month before you arrive at a grandchild's house, send a jar with 30 Hershey's Kisses to represent the number of days until you'll be together. Tell him every day to eat one Hershey's Kiss, and when all the Kisses are gone, you'll be there! For grandparents who've done this, the excitement builds over the 30 days until the children can't wait to eat the last one, knowing that the next day you'll all be together.

Chapter 8

You've Got Mail: Connecting through Letters and Cards

A letter can be a gift of time—
tucked away, saved,
cherished, and passed on.
—Annie Morton

It's interesting how, without realizing it, you can pass on a simple legacy to your grandchild; he or she will pass it on to the next generation in a continuing circle of love. For me, that gift was letter writing. When I was first learning to read and write, my Granny in Houston wrote me a letter. I wrote her back; she wrote me a return letter, and thus began a correspondence that lasted several years until glaucoma took her vision. My first letters were simple—"How are you? I am fine. I love school,"—but grew in content and sometimes included my pictures and poems, and questions about her life.

We only got to see Granny once a year when Mama took us on the train from Dallas to Houston. With a big family of six kids and all the extended family gathered in their small home, there was hardly a chance for me to get a word in edgewise with my grandmother. But writing letters back and forth helped us connect and meant a lot; I was the only one of the six kids who got letters from Granny.

The Value of Snail Mail

Although today we can connect with our grandkids electronically via e-mail, webcam, and text-messaging, children of all ages still love to receive mail. Stamps have gone up in price, but it's still a great investment to send a letter or card.

Since regular contact is key to building relationships, letters can create a special and supportive bond when you live in different places. There's nothing better than encouraging words from Grandma that our grandkids can hold in their hands and tuck away to reread on a bad day. Besides, kids feel very special when a letter or package arrives, addressed to them only. And the handwritten "conversation" might just become a keepsake for later generations to discover.

That's why when my grandchildren started arriving, I made opportunities to write letters and postcards to them. For the grandkids who live close by, I send a colorful postcard when I travel to a different state or country. When they are sick, I send a get-well card; when they finish another year of school, I send a congratulations card.

For my long-distance grandkids, Josephine and Lucy, I keep the postal trail hot between Oklahoma City and Milwaukee. I purchased a pack of postcards for grandkids and send them one by one. I also bought paper with animals all around the sides and printed the letters so Josie could decode the message. I sometimes tuck sticks of sugarless gum, stickers, a dollar, or a batch of Princess Barbie stickers in the envelopes.

> A letter can be read and reread. It calms and soothes the sometimes turbulent waters of life. A letter, once a part of the writer, now becomes a part of the recipient. Outside of our actual presence, a letter is the best physical proof we can offer of our care and concern for others.
>
> —Anonymous

I send Lucy books and write her letters as well, even though she can't read them yet. On the last page of an Elmo book there were words in a big heart under a flap that said, "Elmo loves YOU!" I attached a photo of Lucy and me on that page and wrote in big letters, "Nandy loves YOU TOO!" When her mom read her the book, Lucy said, "NANDY!" for the first time. The picture and message of this simple, colorful book made a connection between us across the miles.

There are so many ways to use the mail to connect with our long-distance grandkids. Just think—a messenger goes to your grandson's or granddaughter's door every day, giving you over 300 opportunities to connect with them through the U.S. Postal Service. Our letters pave the way for their reading and language skills to grow. You may be just the catalyst to start a young person on a lifetime habit of letter writing. As a writer by profession, I look back and see that all those letters Granny and I exchanged planted the seed of a love of writing in me at an early age.

Tips for Connecting through the Mail

Here are some great ways to keep in touch, whether you and your grandkids are only a few minutes or many miles apart. Write on floral stationery or on humorous note cards, illustrate your letters with a cartoon, or jot a note on a travel postcard. With a little thought, the letters and cards you send to your grandkids can be unique, fun, and convey your love.

Here are just a few ideas to get your letters going.

Send balloon messages. Blow up a balloon and write on it in small letters so that your message is impossible to read without blowing up the balloon. A fine-tipped Sharpie works well and won't smear. Make your message something silly or loving. Let the air out, slip the balloon in an envelope, and mail it to your grandchild. He or she will have to blow up the balloon to read the message.

A different way to send a balloon note is to write a message to your grandchild on a small piece of paper, such as, "I miss you!" or "You're special to Nana!" Fold the paper and stick it inside the deflated balloon. When the balloon arrives in the mail, your grandchild blows it up, pops the balloon, and reads the message. If your grandchild is a pre-reader, consider writing a rebus—a message written with pictures and words that young children can decipher.

Make a personalized birthday card. Include a picture of your grandchild on the card, along with some of the things you love most about him.

Send a postcard. A postcard can be written and addressed quickly and only allows you to write a few lines—which is good if you're long-winded! It's also perfect for kids' short attention spans. I've found a terrific bunch of postcards for sending to grandchildren called "Grand-o-grams: Postcards to keep in touch with your grandkids all year-round," and, "More Grand-o-grams." These postcards are available at Target stores and gift shops, and from www.mariannerichmond.com. The Grand-o-grams have Valentine's Day, Halloween, and other holiday post-cards in the collection as well as, "Grandma Loves You!" "You are Special," and other messages. Check out banananana.com for the "Love Notes Booklet," a package of 10 postcards with room on the back for a message.

Send a story. Write a story about something that hap-pened to you recently and send it to your grandchild. Then ask her to tell you a story about the best or funniest thing she experi-enced in her week. At holiday time, send your favorite Christmas story. At Halloween, send a scary story.

Mail cards of encouragement. Joyce, an Illinois grandma, found that sending *Guideposts* cards with an inspiring story and Bible verse is one of the best ways to stay connected with her nine grandchildren who live in different places. Inside, Joyce tells the grandchild how special he is to God and to her. She asks him to let her know how she can pray for him and places a one-dollar bill in each card.

The oldest grandchild is now out of college and on the mission field, four are in college, and the other four are in high school. Joyce has kept the mail coming all through their growing-up years. For these simple expressions of a grandma's love, she's gotten many hugs and thank-yous. The investment she's put into the cards has blessed her flock year after year. Guideposts.com and Christian bookstores, gift stores, and card shops are all good places to find inspirational cards.

Send handmade and purchased coupons. Glenna, a grandma I met recently, sends five-dollar gift cards to McDonald's and coupons to ice cream shops to her five grandkids who are ages six to nine years. To encourage their kindness to siblings, she sends the coupons to one of them at a time with a note to treat their brother or sister to an after-school snack.

You can also make your own coupons. Type or handwrite the coupons and staple them together into a little book. You might include a coupon for a special breakfast out, just Grandma and you; a coupon for a trip to a dollar store; or a coupon for a trip to the zoo. Your grandchildren will have fun redeeming the coupons!

Connecting with our grandkids

through the mail changed the sadness of distance from Texas to Georgia to delight. We sent many, many cards and letters addressed individually to them. They loved mail...their very own. They anticipated getting "goodies" from the big brown UPS truck. At one point our grandchild asked why the big brown truck hadn't been to their house for a long time! Now that one of the grandchildren is old enough to write letters and e-mail, we receive delight. We write back and forth and joy connects Georgia to Texas.

—Shirley and Gabe Utz

Put together a care package. Karen O'Conner suggests surprising your long-distance grandchildren with a care package a few times a year. You can include inexpensive, age-appropriate gifts that let the kids know you're thinking of them. The care package could contain chewing gum (their dentist and parents will thank you if it's sugarless), a CD or DVD, granola bars, candy, homemade cookies, a Bible promise book, or spending money.

Depending on how many grandchildren you have, you can adjust the amount and number of care packages you send. "The important thing is not the money or the items you send," Karen says, "but the fact that you love your grandsons and granddaughters, think about them daily, and want them to know it."

When your grandchild is sick and you can't be there, fill the care package with comforting things such as a package of chicken noodle soup, word games, crossword puzzles, a book by her favorite author to occupy her while she's in bed, or perhaps a soft Webkins animal.

Subscribe to a magazine. Whatever interest your grandson or granddaughter has, there is a kids' magazine to match it. Try *Ranger Rick*, Focus on the Family *Clubhouse*, *National Geographic*, *Sports Illustrated for Kids*, or *Highlights for Children*. You can subscribe to the magazine and it will arrive in your grandchild's mailbox every month without you mailing a thing!

Journaling Across the Miles

Mary Jo Martin wanted to get to know her grandchildren better; she found a way through journal writing and the U.S. mail. She used a black-and-white memo notebook that comes with the top half of the page blank and the bottom half lined. This made it less intimidating for the kids because they could fill the top space with photos or drawings without having to do a lot of writing on the bottom lines. As they get older, the entries get

longer, which has been lots of fun. Journaling across the miles
has proved a great way to connect with each child.

Here is Mary Jo's first letter to her granddaughter.

Dear Katie,

*As you grandchildren get older, it is harder for me to know
what is going on in your lives. So I had an idea! What if we
had a journal together and sent the journal back and forth
between us? We could write about events that are happening in
our lives and even send photos or draw a picture of something
about your life. Some of the grandchildren are too young to be
able to do this, so I have decided to send journals only to those
of you in fourth grade and older.*

*I will enclose a new addressed envelope in the back of your
journal each time I return it so you don't have to worry about
finding another envelope that the journal fits into. The envelope
will have the correct postage for media mail. This way you
can write in the journal and send it yourself.*

*I hope you like this idea and will write me often. Please
keep this journal in the same place each time you receive it so it
won't get misplaced or lost. Maybe a cupboard in the kitchen
or your mom's desk would be a good place to keep it.*

Love, Nana

Special Kinds of Letters

When Shirley and Gabe Utz's grandchildren were young
and lived far away, Grandma and Grandpa sent them cards with
sticks of gum taped inside. On the stick of gum Shirley drew
hair, arms, and legs with jiggly lines so that it looked like the gum
men were "dancing." They also purchased small blank puzzles
with about 25 pieces on which they drew a picture. Then they
separated the pieces and sent them through the mail to be assembled on the other end. They also made "code letters," in which
they gave each letter a number or design, such as drawing an

apple for the letter A, a bee for the letter B, and so on. The children had to figure out what each letter said. Making the letter short helped keep them interested and focused.

There are lots of ways we can use special letters to connect with our grandchildren. Here are a few.

Round-robin letters. When her grandchildren were living in other cities, Dianne Franz thought about the many avenues for communication available in our easy-access world. But she wanted to "talk" with them in the old-fashioned way. For one year she wrote a letter each week to help the grandchildren get a taste of who their grandparents were and what they were about.

This was her format: Each week Diane typed a letter about what was happening in her life and in the world around them. She acknowledged any personal information she knew about each child and always made a big deal about the one having a birthday. The letter was "general" in the sense that she wrote just one letter, but she sent it to both sets of grandkids. She ended with an endearment, a thought for the day, and a riddle for them to solve. At the time she wrote the letters, the children were ages 2 to 12; now they are 6 to 16 and living closer. But the blessings she received from these across-the-miles conversations with her grandkids that year were immeasurable; the letters built a connection that remains to this day.

Birthday Letters. Writing letters to your grandkids on their birthdays is a wonderful way to connect with them, whether you live close and can attend the birthday party, or far away. I've written a few of these to my grandchildren and included the letters with their gifts. But my grandchildren were young and couldn't yet read. They had nothing to keep the letters in, so the letters got thrown away or misplaced during moving or spring cleaning. Fortunately, I saved the letters on the hard drive of my computer, so I'm going to begin again this year to write birthday letters.

Happy Stuff to Put in the Mail

When you write a letter or card, here are some fun things you could send along.

⚝ Stickers (you can buy inexpensive ones or find interesting ones in donation requests from organizations)

⚝ A comic strip from your local newspaper

⚝ Silly rhymes and knock-knock jokes

⚝ Hearts of love: on heart-shaped pieces of paper, write specific traits you appreciate about your grandchild

⚝ Poems you've written or pictures you've drawn

⚝ Quotes that will inspire your grandchild

⚝ Articles and stories from magazines or newspapers in your grandchild's area of interest

⚝ Balloon messages (see instructions on page 94)

⚝ Small, flat things like a stick of gum, a refrigerator magnet, or a "Magic Towel" that becomes a washcloth when wet

⚝ Photos

⚝ A pack of flower seeds to plant

⚝ A riddle or curious question for him or her to solve

That's why I love the idea I've gotten lately from grandmas who write these letters but save them in an album. Frances, a Texas grandma, started writing letters to her grandchildren that journal the cute things they do and say, as well as their time with their grandparents. Throughout the year she keeps notes; then, right after their birthday, she writes them a letter on nice stationery that captures the essence of that year of their life. The letters are handwritten and she keeps them in a three-ring notebook with a plastic sheet protector for each one.

As the grandkids do or say significant things, she jots it down and slips it in the notebook to be included in the annual letter. The notes are important, because in the busyness of life, the special moments can slip away from us. With six grandchildren, it is challenging to remember which child said this or who did that! But she continues this thoughtful letter-writing project, knowing her grandchildren will enjoy reading about themselves in the years to come. She plans to give her grandchildren their notebooks containing all their birthday letters when they come of age.

Baby letters. Some grandparents begin their letter writing even before the child's birth. One night 15 years ago, Peggy Powell got a call from her daughter who told her, "Guess what, Mom? We're pregnant!" Peggy was so excited she couldn't sleep. She got out some notebook paper and wrote a page and a half starting with:

> *Dear Little Baby,*
> *Your mom and dad called tonight with the*
> *news! We don't know if you're a boy or girl.*
> *But we can't wait to meet you and I'm*
> *praying that God will oversee every part of*
> *your development. I love you already.*
> *Grandmommy*

These Are a Few of My Favorite Things

Send a page to your grandchild asking about his or her favorite things. Include a self-addressed, stamped envelope for the child to return the list to you.

What are your favorites?

Teens

Web site _____

Hero _____

Band _____

Book _____

Song _____

TV show _____

Younger children

Food _____

Story _____

Sport _____

Animal _____

Best friend _____

Place you've always wanted to go

_____

_____

During the pregnancy, Peggy wrote the baby four other letters. She included prayers for her grandchild and the parents, then saved the letters for her daughter's baby shower.

Peggy started a spiral notebook when each grandchild was born. She included cute things they said, funny things that happened, and her prayers for them. She feels that someday it will be helpful for the child to know, "At this time and age my grandmother was praying this for me..."

On historical days, Peggy wrote a letter and copied it to include in each grandchild's spiral notebook. At the Millennium, for example, she wrote about the changes happening in the twenty-first century. Peggy has clear page holders for memorabilia such as photos, programs from their school plays, and mementos from visits and trips together.

Story letters. Some grandmas are too busy or have too many grandchildren to keep up 18 different notebooks with detailed accounts of each grandchild's year! Your letter could be as simple as relating one story you remember about your grandchild that year, or a remembrance of a time shared together. It could be a tea party or something funny he or she said, going to Grandparents Day at his or her school, or a story about a big event like a Fourth of July parade you marched in together. Even though the story may be short, you can keep these letters and give them as a collection when your grandchildren graduate

> **My mom and dad live six hours away**
> and have only one grandchild, my two-and-a-half-year-old daughter Anna. They visit when they can, but not as much as they would like. So to stay more involved, they mail Anna simple things, like a whistle, a box of graham crackers, her favorite cereal, or a bubble maker. The postage usually costs more than what's inside, but Anna LOVES it.
> —Laura Myers

from high school. Think about what a treasure you will be giving them: 18 stories of their growing-up years!

Tips on Writing Letters to Grandkids

When you travel, carry a small fabric portfolio with you. Tuck in stamped postcards, notepaper, and envelopes. Include extra stamps for scenic postcards you find along your journey. Send an occasional brochure or photo. In only a few minutes you can write a highlight of your travel day or share an encouraging word.

Keep your letters short, sweet, and simple, especially for younger kids. Make them conversational, as if you're talking with your grandchild.

Have fun not only writing your message, but choosing paper, ink color, and an interesting stamp.

Don't know what to write? Here are some topics: your vacation adventures, your pet's latest mischief, something you love about the grandchild you're writing to, and ideas you're planning for your next time together. They'd also enjoy reading a short story from your childhood or their parents' growing-up years.

Don't forget to include an SASE (self-addressed, stamped envelope) and some blank paper to make writing back easy for your grandchild.

Don't take it personally if your grandchild doesn't reply as frequently as you'd like. Be patient and just know that your letters make his day and build your connection with him!

Ladybug Letters

Every one of Ouida's grandchildren lives in a different state, from the east coast to the west. She keeps the mail going between her home and her grandkids' houses. About once each month she sends a surprise package with a little goodie for each child. Sometimes it is a pack of gum in a regular envelope, sometimes a note on ladybug stationery, because the grandkids call her "Grammiebug." The kids always know it's from her,

Grandma's Supply Shelf

Designate a supply shelf to hold materials that will come in handy when you want to correspond with your grand-kids. Include:

- ✳ Letter-sized envelopes and 9"x12" manila envelopes

- ✳ Stationery, laser and bordered paper, and postcards

- ✳ Three-ring notebooks for saving birthday letters

- ✳ Different-colored pens and stamps

- ✳ Several Priority Mail envelopes with appropriate postage

- ✳ Colorful stickers

because she has ladybug return address labels and puts several ladybug stickers on the envelope.

With eight grandchildren, she has to be practical. She keeps a supply of padded envelopes and a box for storing little treasures to send, from gummy bears to play rings (lead-free jewelry only), small board books, and troll dolls.

She also sends an occasional silly e-card because she likes the fact that her grandkids must interact by clicking on the card's various features. Often they send an e-card back to Grammiebug if Mom is available to help. See Chapter 9 for links to some good e-card Web sites.

Though this grandma often sends consumable things that last a short time, the important thing is that it is mail from Grammiebug and her grandkids know that she is thinking of them when they are apart.

Just for Parents:
How to Help the Mail Connection

✳ Set aside a little time once or twice a month to give your kids writing supplies, including bright paper, pencils, stickers, or markers. Encourage them to write a note or draw a picture to send to their grandparents. Tuck in a recent photo.

✳ If your kids say, "I don't know what to write!" make suggestions, such as, "Why don't you tell about the soccer game Saturday?" or, "Draw a picture of the bunny we saw in the backyard."

✳ When the grandparents send a letter or card, read it to your child and put it up on the refrigerator or bulletin board.

✳ If grandparents send a gift, encourage your child to call or write a thank-you. You'll not only be helping their writing skills improve, but also instilling gratitude and good manners.

With just a little thought and effort, your grandkids will know that they are in your thoughts as you keep the connection going across the miles!

Chapter 9

Connecting Via the Internet and Technology

If nothing is going well,

call your grandmother.

—Italian Proverb

A few decades ago, the only way to connect with loved ones was by phone and mail—and those are still great ways to keep in touch. But today we have the advantage of technology to bridge the distance between grandparents and their grandchildren who live in different places.

Two of Judi's grandchildren are a world away in a Middle Eastern country where her son and daughter-in-law live. Although she sees Anna, two-and-a-half, and Jade, nine months, twice a year, the best way she's found to keep a close connection is through a computer webcam. When all they had was phone communication, they had repeated interference and dropped calls because reception was poor. But with a webcam, they are right there, even with the eight-hour time difference. Here's how it works: Two people at different computers get webcams and microphones and install the same free software. Then they can make video calls to the other computer and speak live, face-to-face!

While Judi has her morning coffee at 5:30 a.m., Marcy, her daughter-in-law, and little Anna call. On her large computer screen, Judi—or Ju-Ju, as her grandkids call her—sees Anna dance across the room and greet her. Later in the day, she reads books to Anna and shows her each picture. When Judi's grandchildren from Waco are in town, all the cousins sit around the computer and talk to Anna. And when Cooper, who is five, reads a book to Anna, her eyes get big and a memory is made. Anna sings them a song; the cousins chime in and sing her songs they've learned in Sunday school.

Judi is not computer-savvy, but she finds this the easiest and best way to keep connected with her grandchildren who live in an Arabic country. What a difference it has made in their communication and their ability to be a part of each other's lives.

Diane, whose eight grandkids live in California, Montana, and Texas, keeps up communication with her teenage granddaughters by cell phone and e-mail. They send brief notes about what is going on in their lives. She responds with bits of news, wisdom, or encouragement, keeping her e-notes brief to ensure that her granddaughters will read them willingly. Since the older girls have cell phones of their own, she gives them a call once in a while or texts a quick message.

Spanning the Distance with Technology

For almost the first two years of Decker's life, his grandparents got to see him regularly because they all lived in the Dallas Metroplex. But when his parents moved him to Minneapolis, Minnesota, my sister Marilyn was bereft. As the "withdrawals" sank in, I suggested that she get a webcam and have Internet chats so she and her husband would be able to see Decker and he could see them. What a difference this has made. Decker would rather chat via webcam than just talk on the phone to his grandparents. Sometimes he does a somersault or shows them a new toy.

One night they called Decker. Before his parents could get to the computer, the little guy (who was in potty-training mode in the bathroom, sans underwear) heard the "ring" and ran to talk to his Ga Ga on the computer. After a few minutes of chatting and hearing his grandma read him a book, he got fidgety and stood up on the computer chair. That's when his grandparents realized he had no pants on! There were lots of chuckles about that. When his grandparents flew up to see him several months later, they had a seamless reconnection. Decker just chatted away as if he'd seen his Ga Ga and DuPaw yesterday. And, in a way, he had.

Yes, technology can be a hassle, but the upside is the ease of connecting across vast distances, especially for grandparents like Sally Matthews whose grandchildren live overseas in East Asia and Macedonia. Communicating by a webcam over the Internet is free, whereas international phone calls can be expensive.

With the help of a webcam, this grandparent has been able to stay close though her grandchildren are growing up on other continents. From Lebanon to Oklahoma, Nevada to San Antonio, and New York to California, grandparents and grandkids are connecting through technology.

> One of life's greatest mysteries is how the boy who wasn't good enough to marry your daughter can be the father of the smartest grandchild in the world.
> —Jewish Proverb

And it's no wonder. Since children and teens tend to be more advanced in using technology than we are, and it's such a natural part of their lives (even for preschoolers), they prefer communicating by webcam to communicating by phone. This is especially true as they grow into pre-teens. As one middle school teacher said, "If you have kids between the ages of 11 and 14, 20 bucks says they're on the Internet right now." Why not join them?

All the advances in technology mean that long-distance grandparenting is easy—after you get the webcam set up and the software downloaded. If you're technically challenged, get a computer-smart friend to help you get everything installed.

However, if this high-tech way of connecting is not your

cup of tea, feel free to send those letters and cards through snail mail; each one makes your grandkids feel extra special.

Webcam Fun

Amy, a young mom who lives in Dallas, has a webcam, as do her parents in Seattle. The grandparents can "see" their grandson regularly, chuckle at his funny expressions, and hear him laugh. Recently Grandma sent her grandson a book and kept a copy of the words so she could read it to him over the Internet while he looked on. It was so much fun that he wanted Grandma to read to him the next night.

One of the most creative ideas I've heard is grandparents and grandkids playing card games via webcam. One set of Jo Anna's grandchildren lives in Tokyo. (Maybe that will make you grateful yours only live in the next state.) Since she's in Texas, the distance creates a huge challenge. They installed a cheap computer camera for about $39, as did their family in Japan.

Every week the grandparents get to talk for free in real time with the children. They play a card game with them, ask them to show their new crafts and schoolwork, and pray with them. When the kids do come home to the States to visit, even the youngest recognizes his grandparents and their voices.

As for the card game, both the grandkids in Japan and their grandparents in Texas have a set of Uno cards. They make up rules for matching and turning over cards to establish winners. They've even invented special rules to play Old Maid. There are other software programs for webcams, so search out the one that works best for you.

Grandparents and grandkids communicating via webcam is the next best thing to being there. Here are some tips for using this technology to build connections.

Get the children talking. Don't do all the talking yourself or they'll tune out—especially young grandchildren.

Plan a few good questions to ask or something to talk about that will engage them onscreen. Share a new joke or riddle each time you call.

Create a story together about a superhero or their favorite fictional character. You start the story and they add an episode, and so on.

Invent a game and play it. One game Marilyn plays is "I'll show you something!" She places something in front of the camera; it might be one of their four little dogs or a flower that just bloomed. Then Decker says, "I'll show YOU something!" He might go and get a carrot or shoe. It's a silly game but he loves it and it keeps him interested. You could play "20 Questions" or "I Spy" with a little adapting. When his little sister Ellis came along a year ago, Marilyn had a great time seeing her first tooth, hearing her first words, and connecting with her, too.

See their creations. Ask your grandchild to show you something he's made or drawn that week. A craft, a picture, or even scribbles are fun to see.

Birthday with Grace

When we realized we would be moving from England to Texas four months before our first child was due to be born, we had some pretty unhappy grandparents on our case. My husband is in the British military so we had no choice in moving, but we had to find some way to bridge the gap caused by several thousand miles.

In the end, we turned to technology and an Internet calling program called Skype. This revolutionized the way we keep in touch with our families. It meant my mom could see my belly expanding every week during the pregnancy, and also see for herself that I was feeling fine. When our daughter Grace was born, they were able to see her very soon after her birth, and have been talking to her that way ever since.

On Grace's first birthday, the first Skype call was to my husband's parents who watched the chaos that only a toddler can cause when opening gifts. They got to see Grace's delight in the boxes as she ignored the gifts, until Daddy built the tricycle they had sent for her. Then they got to see her beaming smile as Daddy sat her on it and pushed her around the room.

Later, as friends gathered to celebrate with us, we called my parents over the Internet and carefully perched the laptop on our fireplace so they had a bird's-eye view. Everyone who came to the party went over and said "hello" to my folks. The grandparents even got to see Grace blow out her candles.

The next day I asked my mom, who is not exactly Bill Gates, what it meant to her to "attend" the party over the Internet. "Oh, Debb," she said, "it gave us great pleasure to be able to join in Grace's birthday party. We were able to see and hear everything exactly as if we were in the room. We could join in the fun and see all the guests and watch the children.

"It was hard to believe that, though we were 5,000 miles away, we could speak to Grace and hear her, even if she was too excited to say much. It was really lovely to be part of a special occasion in a different country!"

Thanks to webcaming, Grace recognizes her grandparents and can interact with them whenever we like. She even does "The Itsy Bitsy Spider" for the webcam! This simple piece of technology has made a huge difference in our family's life.

—Debb Hackett

More Ways to Connect through Technology ✴

In addition to webcaming, there are other ways grandparents are communicating through technology—and you can too.

Post your videos on YouTube. Judi's son Blake, who lives in the Middle East, takes videos of baby Jade playing in a park or Anna picking up Easter eggs and putting them in her basket. Then he posts the videos on YouTube. All this grandma has to do is to click on the link he sends her in the e-mail telling her there's a new video of the grandkids. What a joy it is to see these lively short movies of their life in another part of the world!

Send photos via the Internet. My daughter-in-law Maggie transfers pictures from their digital camera to their Mac, then uploads them to Shutterfly and sends the digital album in one group e-mail to both sets of grandparents as well as aunts and uncles. Instead of getting the pictures a week or two after the birthday or other event, we see them the same day and can order prints of the photos we'd like to purchase.

Send E-cards. Children enjoy getting e-cards, especially the ones that are musical or interactive. The following lists a few of the online sites through which you can send free e-cards. On your busiest days you can let your grandkids know you're thinking about them with only a few clicks. Check out these sites for starters.

✴ Billy Bear's Internet Post Office has free postcards and greeting cards to e-mail to your grandchildren. Visit www.billybear4kids.com.

✴ On 123Greetings.com, click on "kids' cards" and reach out to brighten your grandchild's day.

✴ Click on "Just for Kids" for free e-cards at www.dayspring.com/ecards.

✴ www.Ecards.com has many free cards to send grandchildren. Click on "Earth to Kids," which features original drawings by children, and a variety of cards in categories such as pets, Grandparents Day, holidays, dinosaurs, and "Hippoworks."

✴ You'll also find free e-cards at BlueMountain.com, hallmark.com, and birthdaycards.com.

Play Internet games together. Google "Internet games" to find sites for checkers, chess, card games, Jeopardy, and Wheel of Fortune. There are strategy games, educational games, and even active Wii games that you can play with your grandkids by long distance. These are great for teenagers.

If your grandchild is word-smart, you can use an Internet crossword puzzle program to make a crossword puzzle personalized especially for her. Clues might include upcoming holiday plans, things you love about her, special times together, memories, and favorite activities.

Surprise your grandchildren with a letter recorded on CD or a video of your travels or daily life. Consider buying the family a camera with built-in video so they can make movies and send them to you via the Internet. One family bought their daughters Flip Video cameras—tiny video cameras about the size of an iPod that take up to 60-minute videos. The camera has a built-in USB port that plugs directly into the computer. Software immediately comes up that allows you to e-mail the video instantly. The grandparents receive regular video clips of all their grandchildren. Then they get on the phone and talk about the clip with the kids.

Text messaging is great for teenage grandkids who have cell phones. More and more pre-teens have them as well. It's great for busy, tech-savvy grandparents, because from your BlackBerry or cell phone anywhere in the world you can text message a few words that let them know, "I'm thinking about you," "I love you," "I look forward to seeing you," or whatever short message you want to send.

While living far away in Australia makes it challenging to stay connected with the grandkids in Houston, Texas, we utilize all the technology available to us; that helps the most. First, the favorite "tool" is a VoiP phone (we use Vonage). It's a phone that uses the Internet. That means we have a cordless phone with a handset that rings at our house in Perth, Australia, with a local Houston phone number. We pay $25 per month for unlimited calling. I sound like a commercial, but I cannot express how this one tool has changed the amount and quality of communication with the grandchildren. I can call them every day, and often do. And my daughters can call me from their cell phones just as if it were a local number. We can stay on the line with grandchildren and hear every story in detail without watching the clock or worrying about how much an international phone call costs. We have sat and listened as the baby coos and gurgles, and the two-year-old spins yarns about the ants in the backyard. The only trick is finding the right time to call. With a 15-hour time difference it is tricky, but can be done.

Admittedly, sometimes my chest literally hurts from longing to hold my grandchildren while I'm so far away. But God has been gracious to allow us to connect with today's tools that are inexpensive and easily available. My advice to grandparents living a long way from their kids is to become techno-savvy—quickly!

—Denise Glenn, Founder of "MotherWise"
and author of *Wisdom for Mothers*

Reversing things a bit, when our grandkids are with us, we can ask them to turn off their cell phones for at least part of the time we're together. (Good luck with that, say some folks!) This gives us an opportunity to show our "wired" grandkids how interesting face-to-face conversations can be.

My Family's Web page or blog. If you are up for it, get your tech-savvy teen grandson or granddaughter to help you make a family Web page or blog site. You can even create a family Web page by long-distance. Then invite family members both young and old to contribute news, stories, and pictures.

Connecting by Cell Phone

Of course, talking on the phone is always a great way to connect. All Ouida Phillips's grown children use the same company for their cell phone provider; for a small extra fee each month (approximately five dollars), they get unlimited talk and free minutes. Some of the grandchildren are allowed to use their parents' phones to call their grandparents. To make it easy, they have Grammiebug in the speed dial as number 4. She might call the grandkids before school and pray for their school day or talk about soccer or what they're having for breakfast.

The younger ones often walk around while they talk as they see their parents do, and the conversation will most likely be about what they are seeing. As much as she tries to guide the conversation, Ouida often hears comments like, "Grammiebug, I've got the blue engine leading the train right now," or "It's a spider because I see all eight legs. Can you see them?" Once their mom said they actually held the phone out like a camera so that their grandma could see what they were looking at.

Ouida never knows where the call is coming from. Sometimes when Mom is grocery shopping and little hands are wandering, she calls Grammie to talk to the kids as the cart moves through the aisles. Ouida often gets a call from one of her

Tips on Connecting by Phone

When you can't visit regularly, it helps to call your grandchildren once or twice a week. Here are some helpful things to keep in mind.

✵ You don't have to wait for your grandkids to call you. Give them a buzz!

✵ Be aware of the family's routines and busy schedule so the grandchildren can be available when you call. The 10 minutes before they run out the door to school or soccer practice probably isn't the best time!

✵ When possible, make one call to each grandchild so they feel special and don't argue over who gets to talk more.

✵ Don't worry if younger children don't talk much; just say how much you love them and whatever comes to mind. Some kids are chatty and some are more reserved and quiet on the phone; simply ask them what they're doing. Call after an event or big game and ask them to tell you their favorite thing about it.

✵ Some grandparents call at night and sing a favorite bedtime song to their young grandchildren.

✵ Keep updated by their parents so you know specific things that are going on in their lives, such as basketball tryouts or an upcoming play.

✵ If parents put a photo of you by the phone when the children are talking with you, it helps younger grandkids carry on a conversation.

grandchildren when they're confined to car seats on long car rides. No matter where they are, she loves to hear their sweet voices.

Before the Potters left for Thailand, Granny sang "Bye Baby Bunting, Daddy's Gone a Hunting," over and over to Hunter. Whenever she places a call to Kansas City, they put her on speakerphone and she sings "their song." Two-year-old Hunter always breaks into a big smile. A grandparent's phone call can be like a hug across the miles.

Corresponding by E-mail

You can do interesting things via e-mail, such as sending e-cards as mentioned above. Of course, just sending a regular message is special. But you could also play hide-and-seek by asking the parent to hide treats or surprises in hiding places that you've agreed upon. Send the kids clues in your e-mails.

Have you ever heard of Monk-E-Mail? This is a free program in which you click on hair, clothes, and the background to create the monkey you choose. Then you type a message, which is delivered through the monkey voice you choose. Check out the Web site at careerbuilder.com. Kids get a kick out of receiving a Monk-E-Mail, and creating one takes only two or three minutes of your time.

When communicating by e-mail, remember to:

Keep the message short. Brief, frequent e-mails are better than long-winded ones.

Be aware of grandkids' reading levels and attention spans.

Use symbols like the old-fashioned one for hugs and kisses (XOXOX) or use the "Insert" feature of the toolbar for hearts, faces, and geometric shapes. Create your own symbols to illustrate your message.

Share what you did that day. Your grandkids would love to know if you had a special meal or if you heard from a mutual acquaintance.

Ask questions that don't have a "yes" or "no" reply, but instead are conversation starters. For example, ask, "What was the best part of your day and your worst part?" instead of, "Did you have a good day?"

Attach pictures to your e-mails and ask your grandkids to do the same with a little help from their parents. Digital cameras make it easy to add a photo.

Tell a story. You start a story, one you imagine or one you already know, then e-mail it to your grandchild. He picks up the story and adds an episode, then e-mails it to the next grandchild in another state who shapes the story in her own imaginative way. You can keep passing the story to as many grandkids as you have. When the story ends, share it in a group e-mail so everyone can see the conclusion.

E-mails from our grandkids can encourage us as much as ours encourage them. When Shirley Utz was diagnosed with cancer and began chemotherapy, her 10-year-old grandson Hunter's e-mails became a great source of support and cheer. He continued sending them through her months of treatment. His first e-mail shows his concern.

Hello Mommy and Poppy Oojoos,
*   It's Hunter, and I guess you're wondering how I got your e-mail address and how I got mine! Well, my Dad got me an e-mail address and he gave me Uncle Gary's who gave me yours! Well, I am sorry to here that you are sick with cancer, Mommy Oojoos. I will be praying for you and I might even*

paint you a picture and send it to you in the mail. Hang in there. I know it is hard but you can get through having cancer. I can't wait to see you again! I miss you!

Love, Hunter

Messages like these make us grateful for the wonderful technology that connects our hearts with our grandchildren's, even from long distances.

Connecting through Photos and Memory Albums

Family faces are magic mirrors.
Looking at people who belong to us,
we see the past, present, and future.
We make discoveries about who we are.
—Gail Lumet Buckley

A California grandma who doesn't get to see her two Michigan grandkids as much as she'd like found a terrific way to keep in touch with them. Their mom makes a scrapbook page about what the children are doing at school and sports and sends it to Grandma. The next month or so, Grandma sends the grandchildren a scrapbook page of what's going on in her life. Sometimes it's about a trip she and her husband have taken or just what their life is like during that season. These particular grandparents travel often, and they send along a map of the state or country they're visiting. Last fall, they drove along the entire east coast of the U.S. and sent a wonderful page of travel pictures.

Though they've never lived in the same state as their grandchildren, these grandparents want to have a personal relationship with them; sending scrapbook pages has proved a good way to keep the connection strong. It doesn't take too much time since it's only one scrapbook page sent four or five times a year, and it's lots of fun to put together and receive for both families.

Once this California grandma put together a sheet of photos of her childhood, including pictures of her parents and siblings, the town she grew up in, her aunts and uncles, and schools. She added background details for the pictures, the dates, and the names of the people. Her grandchildren were touched by the page full of memories and looked at it again and again.

Connecting the Past and the Present

     Photographs are a marvelous way to connect with our loved ones—especially our grandchildren. I've loved photographs all my life. When I was five years old, I got my first Brownie camera and saved up the money to buy a photo album. I still have the old album with its thin, black pages and brown cover, which is coming apart; I cherish the photos I saved there. One of the sweetest gifts my dad's mother, Grandmother Heath, ever gave me was an invitation to go through a box of her cherished old photos that dated back to her childhood and early marriage. Knowing I was working on my album, she let me pick out my favorites to keep in my collection. There was a photo of my great-grandparents, whom I never met, photos of my father as a boy, my uncle in his Army uniform in World War II, my Aunt Earlene as a Hollywood star, and many other things I got to see for the first time.

> No cowboy was ever faster on the draw than a grandparent pulling a baby picture out of a wallet.
> —Anonymous

     Because my paternal grandparents, father, and aunt all died when I was young, those photos have been treasures I've cherished my whole life. Knowing from an early age that life was brief, I wanted to somehow capture the moments that seemed to flee so fast and to remember the people I loved. So I continued taking pictures of siblings, family, and friends. When our children and grandchildren came along, what fun I had photographing them! (Except, perhaps, when one of them whined, "Mom, not another picture!") Actually, now that they are adults, they're glad I took the photos and recorded their growing-up years.

I've found that even my youngest grandchildren notice the photos we have around the house and respond to them—especially photos in which they appear. Early childhood experts say that from the age of two, children show interest in photos we've framed, put in albums, or placed around the house. Since repetition is a major way they learn, children often want to look at a favorite photo album or picture on the wall many times.

The Alphabet Book: Story of Your Life

Cynthia Huffmyer has found that the best way to stay connected with her grandchildren is with an Alphabet Book she makes and gives them on their second birthday. Not only does the ABC book help them learn the alphabet, it's been a real key for the grandkids who live in Arizona to get to know their relatives—and, of course, their grandparents in Oklahoma. They do take time, but Cynthia enjoys making the ABC books and especially loves seeing how they build relationships between her grandkids and the family. She does the project as economically and simply as possible, because the photos are the focus. Her goal isn't to create an elaborate work of art, but to chronicle the story of the children's young lives so far and help them learn their ABCs.

Here's how she does it. Cynthia gets a cardboard photo box; when she takes pictures, she stores the ones she might use for an alphabet book in the box. At family gatherings, she makes a point to take a picture of every family member with the grandchild.

When it's time to start the book, she takes 26 pieces of white typing paper and spreads them out on the floor: A, B, C, D, E, F, and so on to Z. For A, she fills the page with pictures of her granddaughter Holden with her aunties and other relatives whose names start with an A. She adds a picture of an apple (a favorite fruit) and other "A" things that Holden likes.

For B, she puts a picture of Uncle Barrett, a basketball, a

balloon, and a bike. Under the pictures she writes the name of the person and identifies the event. For H, she spreads out photos of her granddaughter doing things she loves: sliding down a slide and acting silly with her baby brother. H is also the beginning letter of the family name, Huffmyer, so she puts in a picture of the whole family.

N is for Nanny—that's what the grandkids call her—so she includes pictures of things she and Holden do together, along with a "night, night" photo of Holden in pajamas. The O page has Holden in an Oklahoma State University outfit and a University of Oklahoma cheerleader costume. Q has a photo of Holden with a crown on, playing queen. The S page has a picture of Holden and Santa. The U page has a photo of Holden with an umbrella and a photo of her upside down. V has all kinds of vacation pictures. Y has a picture of Holden eating ice cream with the words "Yum, yum" written below the photo. For Z, there's a real zipper and photos of Holden at the zoo with animals she saw.

After all the pages have pictures on them, Cynthia gets out her colored backing sheets: polka dot pages and pink, girly backgrounds for her granddaughter's books; and blue, red, and green for her grandboys' books. The very first page she creates is a "Happy 2nd Birthday" sheet, complete with confetti, balloon stickers, and pictures of the grandchild. Every page has its own colored backing with the pictures arranged on it.

During the year, she collects butterfly and flower stickers for the girls and train and fire engine stickers for the little guys. Each of the grandchildren has a favorite thing, an attachment to something—Tate loves Snoopy so she includes pictures of him with his stuffed Snoopy dog and Snoopy stickers. Lawson's thing is Mickey Mouse, so stickers of Mickey decorate some pages. She also cuts out the Wiggles from their CD cover and Shrek and Nemo (two favorite movie charac-

> Photos tell the story
> of your life.
>
> —Unknown

ters) from fruit snack boxes—a good way to get a colorful picture without buying something extra!

She attaches the photos with scrapbook adhesive squares or acid-free glue. Then she glues a three-inch-tall alphabet letter on each page. Sometimes she crops pictures around the grandkids' heads and puts them on a square of backing paper.

When her grandkids receive their ABC album, they love looking at the pictures and having Nanny or their parents read it to them. It has really helped them learn their alphabet and build letter recognition, but ultimately serves an even bigger purpose: to connect the child to his or her grandparents and the whole family.

More Ways to Connect with Your Grandkids through Photos and Memory Albums

Let your grandkids take you home. Frame a picture of both grandparents, or of you and your grandchild. Send it home with her when she leaves, or place it on her bedside table when you visit next.

One grandma I know wasn't able to meet her grandbaby right away due to the long distance between them. So she sent her daughter a big photograph of Grandma and Grandpa to put near the changing table. Babies are fascinated by faces. Because she saw the photo of her grandparents every time her diaper was changed, their faces became familiar.

When Cheri Potter and her husband taught in an international school in Thailand, Cheri had a photo taken with Audrey, their only grandchild at the time, before they left. She put it in a soft fabric frame and made it very special when she gave it to Audrey. At bedtime one night she said, "This is how Granny and Granddad can sleep with you. You just lie down and look at us together with you and remember what fun we had. Then say a prayer for us in the land of the elephants, and stick the photo under your pillow and we will sleep with you!"

When Cheri and her husband arrived in Thailand, their

daughter Christy e-mailed to tell them what went on that first morning after they'd left. Christy was making up her daughter's bed and found the framed photo under her pillow. Christy cried, then Cheri cried when she read the e-mail. But it worked, and in the months that followed Audrey loved "sleeping" with her grandparents.

Guess who loves you. If you aren't inclined to make a photo book from scratch, you can purchase colorful ones in baby departments. One by Sassy called Who Loves Baby? has plastic photo sleeves for four-by-six pictures. I often give these adorable books with baby shower gifts; because the books are soft enough to chew on safely, they're ideal for teething babies. And, they help babies recognize the faces of their grandparents and others who love them. Due to the fact that there are no such baby photo books available in Thailand, grandma Cheri instead took a photo of herself and Grandpa, backed it with poster board, and laminated it. She mailed the photo to their one-year-old grandson Hunter in the States so he could hold it and look at it.

Refrigerator gallery. When my grandkids come over, they usually head for the kitchen, not only for a snack, but to look at the picture gallery on the front of the refrigerator. They search for their photos as well as new pictures I might have added. They especially love silly pictures—photos of themselves when they were babies, and a shot of all six grandkids together at a holiday "Cousin Party." Someone once said that if God had a refrigerator, your picture would be on it. Make sure your grand-kids' pictures are on your refrigerator! If you want the refrigera-tor collection to look orderly, you can buy magnetic frames and put one grandchild in each frame.

Magnet photos. You can make your own refrigerator mag-nets to display photos of your grandkids and pets. And you can slip these in an envelope to display on their mom's refrigerator as

Alphabet Book Supplies

Cynthia keeps her eyes open for materials when craft stores have half-price sales. You can also find the supplies at large discount stores and scrapbooking shops:

✴ White typing paper

✴ Photographs of your grandchild with various family members and pets, and shots of them participating in activities

✴ Sticker sheets of things such as balloons, animals, favorite cartoon characters, princesses, and fire engines

✴ Three-inch-tall bright colored, basic letters (like preschool teachers use)

✴ Acid-free glue and/or scrapbook adhesive squares to secure photos

✴ Colorful stickers

✴ Photo-safe labeling pen

✴ Scissors

well. Magnetic sheeting can be found in craft and photo stores and on the Web. You just pull off the protective backing paper and stick on the back of the picture. Be careful—it sticks like crazy, so you get one shot at placing it! Magnetic sheeting comes in different sizes and is inexpensive: I found a 10-pack of wallet-sized self-adhesive magnets for $2.70.

Puzzling grandparents. Have someone take a photo of both Grandma and Grandpa, and get a five-by-seven or eight-by-ten print of the picture. Use glue stick or scrapbook adhesive to adhere the photo to a piece of cardboard. Draw puzzle shapes with a pencil on the back of the cardboard, then cut the puzzle pieces apart. For little ones, make the pieces bigger; for older grandkids, cut them smaller so the puzzle will be more challenging. Put the puzzle pieces in an envelope on which you've written, "Guess who LOVES YOU? Put the puzzle together and you'll find out!"

Photo calendar. At copy shops such as Kinko's or on Internet sites such as Shutterfly, Snapfish, and Creative Memories, you can make photo calendars with pictures of you and the grandkids doing things together. Give them as gifts for Christmas and birthdays. Grandkids can post the calendar on their bulletin boards and mark the dates they will be visiting your home and the dates you will travel to their house.

Grandkids' Do-it-yourself Memory Book. Older grandkids may like to "do it themselves" when it comes to making memory albums. One summer when my granddaughter Caitlin, then eight, was visiting us from St. Louis, I took her to the Oklahoma City Zoo. Instead of wielding the camera as I usually do, I gave her my Sony digital camera and told her she was the photographer of the day. "Take pictures of your favorite animals and scenes," I said. Caitlin loved this. I gave her a little notebook and pen to write down the animals' names and anything interesting she wanted to jot down about them to put in her book later.

> Life is not about significant details, illuminated in a flash, fixed forever. Photographs are.
>
> —Susan Sontag

We had a great time walking around the zoo, riding the train, talking about the animals, and eating snacks on that hot July day. She took pictures of pink flamingos, striped tigers, monkeys hanging from their tails, unusual butterflies, and an acrobatic seal.

When we got home that afternoon, I had everything she needed to make a memory book spread out on a plastic cloth covering the dining room table: a small, white hardback book, different colors of backing paper, scrapbook adhesives, scissors, and a portable photo printer. I put the memory stick in the photo printer, pushed a few buttons, and off we went! While I printed out the photos, Caitlin designed and drew a cover for her book. She put the photos in the arrangement she wanted and attached one to each page; then, below the pictures, she wrote the animal's name and something about it.

When her mom and dad picked her up that evening, she had a completed memory book of our day at the zoo to take back to St. Louis!

Quick-to-Make Mini-Albums

Mini-albums are doable because they are small projects—a week's worth of photos from one visit, rather than a year's worth. I've made mini-photo albums for each of our grandchildren when I visited Josephine in Hawaii or when she and baby sister Lucy were in Milwaukee. I've made them for Caitlin and Caleb in St. Louis, and when they've visited our home. Some of them I made in small four-by-six-inch albums purchased from Target, Old Navy, or hobby stores. I added narration, titles, and stickers as I had time.

A grandparent who lives an hour away from her grandchildren has an individual date with each grandchild every year. One time she and her granddaughter went to a play her friend was starring in. They went out to a fancy dinner after the play, walked around to see the glittery lights in downtown Grand Rapids, and both took pictures. The simple mini-album of their evening provided wonderful memories of a special time together.

Scrapbooking with Grandkids

Scrapbooking can bring generations together and connect your hearts and memories. When your grandchildren visit or you have a family gathering, put out a big table with photos from the past and present, newspaper clippings, old family letters, and memorabilia. In a box or small tote provide scrapbooking materials and fun add-ons such as rubber stamps and stickers.

Here are some tips for a successful Scrap-a-Thon:

- Start small. Don't try to do a whole album in one sitting; aim for completing just a few pages.

- Sort the photos by year, holiday, or special events, and put them in zip-top bags.

- Pick a theme for each page.

- Crop pictures, but avoid cutting an antique photo; instead, make a copy and use it, preserving the old picture.

- To help tell the story, add titles, dates, people's names, and comments.

For long-distance grandparents, there's no better way to share your life and stay in touch with your grandkids than through sharing photos and making albums. Be creative and dream up your own crafts involving photos!

Connecting through Arts and Crafts

Better a creative mess
than tidy idleness.
—Unknown

Each year when her grandchildren visit her in Indiana, Kathy Carlson has a craft project all ready for them to do. From toddlers to teenagers, the five granddaughters and one grandson sit around a big table and get to work. One year they made friendship bracelets from macramé and beads. Another year they made their own fleece blankets with fringes. They've painted sweatshirts, done cross-stitch pictures and framed them, painted clear glass ornaments, and made jewelry. The big body pillows they made together one year are favorites to use while lying on the floor watching television or snuggling on their beds while doing homework.

When their hands are busy, the grandchildren are more open and relaxed. As they tie fringe knots or paint beads for necklaces, they catch up with each other and their grandma about school experiences, their friends, and goings-on. It's a great time for them to see that grandmas can make mistakes too; kids tend to put them on a pedestal, thinking they can do no wrong. Kathy points it out when she makes a mistake in crocheting or sewing so the grandkids can see that she can laugh about it, fix the mistake, and not get angry or frustrated—a great lesson! She displays the creations she has fixed so that even the imperfect stitch or brushstroke becomes part of the uniqueness of the craft. Handling mistakes this way is an important lesson that the grandkids can carry into their schoolwork, sports, and everyday lives.

Some of the children really get into the craft projects and want to do more. Others aren't quite as interested. But the opportunity to try something new, do it together, and learn new things is a gift.

Kids today are so busy. Most of their parents have packed schedules and neither time nor inclination to do crafts. But doing a project has proved to be something Kathy's grandkids look forward to every year, and it's a great

> It's not a mess.
> It's a work of art.
> —Unknown

way to connect with their grandma. When the grandkids take home something they've created themselves, they feel a great sense of pride. They often display their crafts on a shelf in their bedrooms; they've even taken the body pillows and fleece blankets to college. Just being able to say, "I made this," is a joy.

Pick and Choose! ✹

The ideas in this chapter are not meant to be done in one visit, or even one summer! Instead, let me encourage you to choose a project that works for you, your house, and your grandchildren—perhaps one for a visit, a holiday gathering, or a Cousin Camp. In this chapter, you'll find enough ideas to last for years. Some are easy projects; others need more supervision. You don't have to be a crafty grandparent to do most of them. I'm certainly not artistically gifted; I find crocheting and knitting difficult. But coloring in a coloring book—I can manage that!

Let's get started and see what creativity we can stir up with our grandkids. First, we've got to get together some art and craft supplies. Start small, look for sales, and add to your materials as you go and as your grandkids grow.

Tips for Making Crafts with Your Grandkids ✻

Here are some helpful tips Kathy Carlson has learned through the years for doing crafts with grandkids.

Get the materials beforehand. Put the items needed for the project into a kit so it's all ready for each grandchild to use. When they have everything they need in big zip-top bags, it is easier for them to work on the project and complete it. (When I asked Kathy where she buys fleece blanket kits, she told me that Jo-Ann Fabrics, Hancock Fabrics, and other sewing stores carry them.)

Have one completed project for them to see. When you've done the craft, you know the pitfalls and can better coach them as they work on it. And when kids get to see what the finished project looks like before they start, they are more motivated to put effort into it.

If the project uses fabric, ask your grandkids before they arrive what colors and patterns they prefer. Or, have a selection on hand and let them pick their favorites.

Don't aim for perfection. Remember, it's the process, not the project that's important. It's the fun of doing the craft and the satisfaction of completing it rather than making a perfect product that matters. When you make mistakes, let your grandkids see how you handle it. When they get frustrated or stuck at a certain point, instead of letting them quit, show them how to fix the mistake and keep going.

Keep it fun, enjoy the conversation around the table between cousins, and remember that the focus is not only helping them make a craft, but also connecting with your grandkids.

Providing Raw Materials for Creativity

Diane, an Oklahoma potter and artist, says that if we provide children with materials and a place where they can work so they're not getting scolded for making a mess, they'll use the materials to create or draw something.

I always admired the organized way in which my long-time friend Ann provided the raw materials for arts and crafts for her grandchildren when they were preschoolers. She didn't get everything at once, but bought the items as she found them on sale at craft stores so it wasn't a big investment. She collects some normal household items, such as craft sticks, foam meat trays, and scraps of ribbon. Free greeting cards and stickers come in envelopes from charities and organizations she supports.

She purchased a set of clear plastic stackable drawers and organized the art and craft materials in each compartment. When her twin grandsons came over to see her, they almost always wanted to make something or paint a picture.

Here are some of the items Ann gathers for arts and crafts.

✷ craft sticks and toothpicks

✷ brads

✷ stickers of birds, animals, and seasonal things

✷ rulers

✷ kid scissors

✷ a stapler

✷ glue sticks

✷ old photos

✷ a watercolor set and washable tempera paints

✷ pipe cleaners, feathers

✳ zip-top bags filled with pieces of ribbon

✳ stamps and ink pads

✳ crayons, markers, and colored pencils

✳ small paintbrushes and foam paintbrushes

✳ an oilcloth table cover

✳ paper: construction and manila paper, one large pack and one letter-sized pack; old wallpaper samples; and a big roll of white paper from educational supply stores—it's fairly inexpensive and will last forever

✳ paper towel tubes, toilet paper rolls, and long brown gift wrap rolls; they can become anything from light sabers to a fairy's wand

> ### My mother has 18 grandchildren.
> She is so connected with all of them. Over the years she has taught art to them once a week. She set up card tables and taped paper on the underside. They all became Michelangelos as they lay on their backs and painted on the "ceiling."
>
> —Julie Miller

Craft Table 🍁

The art materials I had gathered for my grandkids always seemed to be spread over different places after one of their visits: in a cabinet here, on a desk in the sun porch, or laying on the kitchen counter. This spring I decided to designate a grandkids' craft table. I covered an old but sturdy trestle table with a one-dollar yellow tablecloth and bought small, clear bins to house the materials: pipe cleaners in one drawer, markers in another, and kid scissors, tape, and stapler in another. One houses small brown paper bags, buttons, yarn, feathers, sequins, and scraps of fabric for making puppets. There are wiggly eyes and small colored pom-poms for making people. I added the construction paper, notebooks, and paints, but left room on the table for the children to draw and make whatever they liked.

Sometimes I draw with them, and sometimes they get into a project by themselves. Five-year-old Luke loves to cut out paper; he made a colorful collage out of orange, green, and yellow construction paper cut in various shapes. The grandchildren can just come in, head for the craft table when they are in the mood, and color, paint, or create something all on their own—which I display on the kitchen windowsill or on the refrigerator.

This week Noah and Luke came in and saw the craft sticks. Things were quiet for a while, and then they came out to show us their creations. Luke made a house, glued on small bright-colored pom-poms, painted the sticks, and said, "This is a house decorated in Christmas lights." Noah made a painted sign with flowers. The last time Caitlin was here, she decorated a foam visor with stick-on flowers and letters to spell her name.

I also have folders, each in a different color, labeled Luke, Caleb, Noah, Caitlin, Josephine, and Lucy, to store the drawings and collages they make after they've been displayed.

Your supply place could be "grandma's craft drawer" filled with odds and ends that would inspire a child to create something.

> **I've always had a place in my home** for my grandchildren where they can do special things they don't get to do at home, like painting, working with clay, scrapbooking, or making jewelry. Each of them thinks that place is just theirs! After a memorable trip with my eight-year-old granddaughter last year, I printed pictures and set out everything she would need to create a scrapbook all her own. Then she could tell the story of the vacation using her book.
>
> —Julie Miller

If arts and crafts aren't your cup of tea but you'd still like to do projects when you're with your grandkids, check out www.creativekidsathome.com. You can sign up for a free monthly newsletter that offers all kinds of creative ideas for kids including crafts, activities for parties and special days, and links to similar Web sites.

Art Activities: An Inexpensive Potpourri of Ideas

Creating art together can make a positive connection with your grandchildren because you're engaging in an active, hands-on developmental process. Besides having lots of fun, you'll be helping build their creativity, eye-hand coordination, and small motor development. Here are some ideas to get you started.

Wall of fame. Get out crayons and markers, roll out shelf paper, and let your grandkids create their own summer scenes, dinosaurs, monsters, and funny people.

Crazy for beads. If your grandkids are little and you want to avoid choking hazards, get big plastic beads to string into a necklace. For older kids, there are all kinds of glass beads, from inexpensive to fancy ones. Buy stretchy plastic beading cord that you finish with a simple knot.

T-shirt paint shop. Using water-based fabric paints, let your grandchild design her own T-shirt. If several are together for a holiday or Cousins Camp, they could all have the same color T-shirt to decorate in their individual way. There are many fun tie-dye T-shirt kits. Fourth of July T-shirts are fun to make using red, white, and blue puff paint, sequins for the girls, and glitter. Or, cut sponges in different shapes to dip in paint and press on the T-shirts. Grandkids can glue on lace, buttons, ribbon, jewels, or whatever you have.

Create a hideaway. Save a large appliance box, provide paints or markers, and let the children create a colorful playhouse or reading hideaway. Inside, put a flashlight, a pillow, and a few good books.

You can also cut the bottoms off of large cardboard boxes and connect them with duct tape to make a tunnel, house, or fort. Cut small, square openings for the windows and let them go wild decorating the hideaway in any way they can dream up. Then they can read or play in it.

Stamping fun. Get rubber stamps and washable tempera paint. Use little foam paintbrushes to spread the paint lightly on the surface of the stamp. Grandkids can use the stamps to make pictures, their own gift wrap, or greeting cards.

Very Cool Art Materials

✧ Craypas are a combination of pastels and crayons. Kids love the rich, vivid colors.

✧ Real clay is actually very inexpensive—around eight dollars for 25 pounds. You could share the clay with a few friends and keep your portion in the plastic bag inside a bucket where it won't dry out. With some cookie cutters, a garlic press to make hair or a lion's mane, and your grandkids' busy hands, they can make animals, people, houses, angels, or monsters. If you have a friend with a kiln, you can fire the clay creation and paint it, but you don't have to—it's the process of working in clay that counts. As an alternative, you could buy self-hardening clay that comes iin smaller quantities and can be painted when dry.

✧ Inexpensive cardboard boxes or frames. These are available at hobby stores and have lots of uses: Have your grandkids make a gift by gluing on shells or bright sequins. Painting and decoupage are other options. When the unique frame is finished allow your grandchild to choose a favorite picture to go in it.

✴ For young grandchildren, a new product is Crayola washable poster and craft paint, which comes in big squeezable tubes. It's ideal for little hands.

✴ Make a trip to an arts and crafts store or hobby shop and you'll find new products every time. On one trip, I found a wooden birdhouse kit, Wikki Stix (colorful wax-covered yarn), and a half-price "Creative Coloring Castle" kit that would keep the kids busy for quite a while.

✴ A Kiddie Art Apron is handy but it's even cheaper to get an old T-shirt to protect their clothes! Their parents will appreciate this.

✴ Origami paper, used to fold birds, animals and all kinds of beautiful things, is available in book form with directions, or in smaller packages.

✴ From glitter glue to fancy feathers, the list of materials goes on and on. See what materials you find, and enjoy creating something with your grandkids!

Sidewalk art gallery. Here's one of the most entertaining and easiest art activities you can do with children. Get a tub of large, bright colors of sidewalk chalk, take the grandkids out on the driveway, and let them draw shapes, animals, letters, and numbers to their hearts' content. Have them lie down, then trace around their bodies with the sidewalk chalk. Let them fill in the eyes, nose, mouth, hair, and clothes.

Puppet fun. You can buy manufactured puppets, but it's even more fun to let your grandkids make their own. They can create paper-bag puppets with buttons for the eyes and nose and yarn for hair. With white glue, attach feathers or rickrack for trim.

Sock puppets are also fun to make from Grandpa's old socks. Use wiggly eyes, yarn hair, and scraps of fabric and ribbon for trim. To make fancy puppets, add sequins or sew on beads. Once the puppets are finished, encourage your grandkids to use them in a puppet play.

Magazine collage. Save a stack of magazines and get them out when your grandkids visit. Buy different colors of poster board and hand them out. Set the timer for 30 minutes or less, depending on the age of your grandchildren. Tell them to rip

---

A Thanksgiving Tradition

While the turkey is cooking and food is being prepared in Grandma's kitchen, Gretchen Beene, her five children, and all the family members present make a "Thankful Tree." They cut out a huge tree from brown paper and attach it to the wall. Then everyone writes on it what they're thankful for from that year. The last Thankful Tree had written on it, among many other things:

✡ "I'm thankful for Nanny and Grandpa because they let me come in their bed when it's dark outside and I'm thankful God put two babies in Mommy's tummy."
—Samantha, whose twin siblings were born
a few months later.

✵ "I am thankful for Nanny and Grandpa because they let me eat some of the cake and cookies before they are baked. I'm thankful Grandma is staying at my house for my birthday."
—Kate

✵ "I'm thankful for donuts and bubble baths and bike rides and deer and flashlights."
—Jimmy

✵ "I am thankful for the Internet because without it no Christmas shopping would get done, and for e-mail and how it makes it easy to stay in touch with friends and family. And for bright, crisp, crystal-clear, blue-sky days with crunchy leaves."
—Mom

The thank-yous covered the brown paper tree as this family continued their tradition of gratitude. Isn't that what family is all about? Each day is a gift, and as we gather in our kitchens and around our tables, giving thanks is a tradition to pass down across generations.

out pictures they like. They can use kid scissors, but ripping is faster and more fun. Have them glue the pictures on the poster board with a glue stick. When the timer goes off, go around and let everyone tell why they picked the pictures on their poster. Why did these things appeal to them? Though this is an easy activity, it can stimulate great conversation from the youngest to the oldest. Let them take their posters home and put them up in their rooms.

If Grandparents Are Doing It

In things pertaining to arts and crafts, my friends and I have found that if grandmas and grandpas are doing it, the kids love to join in and do what they do. If we are doing clay, they want to do it too. If we are making Christmas decorations or painting a picture, they say, "Me too!" If Grandpa's making a wooden birdhouse in the garage, the children want to wield the hammer.

Whether it's making simple paper chains, stamping, or drawing, arts and crafts are a vehicle for connecting and communicating, giving our grandkids a chance to express their creativity, and having fun at the same time. Do it informally. Don't aim for perfection or performance; let your grandkids know that what they create is valuable and appreciated because it's an expression of them.

Chapter 12

Someone's in the Kitchen with Grandma

*It's loving and giving
that makes life worth living.*
—Unknown

Throughout her 88 years of life, Flossie greeted her new neighbors with freshly baked cinnamon rolls. If anyone moved within three blocks of her home, she walked her petite four-foot eight-inch self down the road to greet them with a smile, some friendly chatter, and her famous rolls. Fortunately Flossie passed her generous spirit and recipe on to her daughter, granddaughter, and great-granddaughter Shenae.

Shenae can never bake a cinnamon roll without thinking of her great-grandma in a red-checkered apron mixing, kneading, and rolling out dough. With infinite patience, Shenae's greatgrandma taught her the fine points of making mouthwatering cinnamon rolls. Flossie created a beautiful memory and legacy—one Shenae has passed on to her own children.

Perhaps making cinnamon rolls isn't your specialty, but you have another recipe or baked good that you make to the delight of other people. Are you famous for your chicken and dumplings or homemade mac and cheese? This may seem simple and small to you, but passing the recipe along to your grandkids and teaching them how you make it could prove to be a lovely memory and a transfer of family history as well.

Bridging the Generations through Cooking Together 🍁

Like Shenae, lots of us remember special foods when we think of a beloved family member. When I eat chicken tetrazzini, I think of my great-aunt Bess who made a large vat of it when our family of eight descended upon her home on Sundays for dinner many years ago. I remember Grandmo's, my husband's grandma's, airy-light angel food cake she made every Easter and decorated with little chicks and jelly beans. His paternal grandmother's secret recipe for shortcake was passed down as well; we all love to eat it piled with strawberries and whipped cream in the summer.

Besides the joy of eating something warm and yummy, food can bridge the generations and connect a child to his or her family history. And when children get to help prepare it, they feel part of a grown-up activity. Buy your grandchildren their own cookbooks and invite them into your kitchen.

Connie, who has grandkids in Kansas and California, has a stepstool in her kitchen. Whenever she begins to make something, the grandchildren who are visiting—beginning with the two-year-olds—scoot the stool over to the counter and say, "I want to help!" Their favorite things to make are Toll House chocolate chip cookies. Using the recipe on the bag, Connie lets them measure all the ingredients, turn on the mixer, and add the eggs. They especially love dumping flour and sugar in the bowl and packing down the brown sugar.

With families living at a breakneck pace, many mothers are so busy that they don't have time to cook with their children. Ordering take-out and eating out have become the norm. Inviting kids into the kitchen may invite a mess. As Connie says, "I have a lot more patience than I had when I was a mother, and

Granma Flossie's Cinnamon Rolls

Soak 1 cake (or 1 package or 2 tsp.) yeast in ½ cup lukewarm water and set aside. Beat 1 egg and set aside. In mixing bowl, combine the following and mix well:

- ½ cup butter
- ½ cup sugar
- 1½ tsp. salt
- 1 cup boiling water

Cool the mixture, then stir in 1 cup flour. Add yeast, egg, and 2½ cups of flour. Mix well with mixer or wooden spoon until dough is smooth. Cover with plastic wrap and let dough rise until double.

Divide dough in half and roll out in a ⅓-inch-thick rectangular shape. Spread melted butter on top and sprinkle with cinnamon and sugar to cover dough. Roll up lengthwise as tightly as possible and slice. Place slices in a cake pan that has been rubbed with butter. Let rise until double.

Bake in a 350° oven for 15-20 minutes or until golden brown. While rolls are baking, make frosting: In a saucepan, mix

- ⅓ cup butter
- 2 cups powdered sugar
- 1 tsp. vanilla
- a few drops of milk to desired consistency

Mix over low heat until smooth. Remove rolls from oven, and while still warm, frost with icing.

the mess doesn't bother me." If a teaspoon or even a bowl of flour falls on the floor, she doesn't make a big deal out of it. The grandchildren learn that when they make a mistake, it's not the end of the world. They also learn how to measure, mix, and follow a recipe. Learning to follow directions helps them in the classroom. But the conversation over the mixing bowl is priceless.

When Connie's California granddaughter Ashlyn was in the second grade, she drew a picture of a grandmother—with glasses and brown hair just like hers. Under it she wrote, "Grandmas are special and the best thing about mine is she makes delicious cookies with me." Now Ashlyn is 11 years old and likes to bake by herself.

Besides the fact that the child is doing something other than watching TV, when we cook with our grandkids they get to see how some random-looking ingredients can turn into something tasty. We share about good nutrition; they learn responsibility from helping clean up the kitchen. I've never met a kid who didn't like to crack eggs, mix, and pour. And while we let them do these things, we can visit and talk.

Easy, Whimsical Recipes to Make with Grandkids 🍁

Animal pancakes. I don't know any kids who don't like pancakes, especially in animal shapes. To make them, prepare a healthy pancake batter and then drop by spoonfuls onto a hot griddle in any of these shapes: for a dog, drop one big spoonful of batter for the body and smaller drops for the head and ears; for Tony the Turtle, drop a big spoonful of batter with six small drops for the head, ears, feet, and a long, thin turtle tail; for a bunny, make two round dollops for the head and body and two long shapes for the ears; use raisins or blueberries for the eyes. Use your imagination to create dinosaur pancakes, zebras, bears, and other favorite animals.

> Grandmas are moms with lots of frosting.
> —Anonymous

A new twist on an old classic. Make the original recipe for Rice Krispie treats. Melt three tablespoons of butter in a large pan on low heat. Add four cups of mini-marshmallows and stir until melted. Remove from heat and add six cups of Rice Krispies. Stir until the cereal is well coated. Press into a greased cookie sheet.

Then the fun begins! Before the mixture is cooled and hard, use whatever cookie cutters you have to make hearts, stars, or gingerbread men. Then decorate with red hots, sprinkles, frosting, or whatever is handy. Cool and enjoy eating the same day. You won't have any trouble getting rid of them!

Ants on a log. There are lots of no-bake, healthy foods you can make with your grandchildren. One my granddaughter Caitlin taught me is "Ants on a Log." Take washed, cut celery stalks and let the kids use a butter knife or plastic knife to fill them with peanut butter or cream cheese. Add a row of raisin "ants," and enjoy!

Happy wheels. This is a more substantial item to make for lunch. Wrap six small flour tortillas in paper towels and heat them in the microwave on high for 30 seconds. Keep them covered so they won't dry out. Spread one tablespoon of light cream cheese over one side of each tortilla. Top with lettuce and thinly sliced ham. Over the ham, spread another tablespoon of cream cheese. Roll up tightly to form a log. Use a serrated knife to cut the logs into one-inch slices. Place in an airtight container and chill for several hours. This recipe makes lots of happy wheels to enjoy for a picnic.

Cupcake cones. Prepare a cake mix according to the directions, using any flavor, and fill ice-cream cones about half full with cake batter. Stand the cones in a muffin pan and bake for 20-25 minutes. Cool and frost, then sprinkle colored sugar on top for a very special treat. This makes a lot of cones—24 to 36—so share them with others!

ABC sandwiches. All you need is peanut butter and your grandkids' favorite jelly, plus a box of alphabet cereal. After spreading the bread with peanut butter and jelly, let the children use alphabet cereal to spell their names or write a message on top of their sandwiches. If they can't write yet, let them stick the letters on any way they want!

Play in the dirt. Making this treat is a fun snacktivity. Crush a package of chocolate sandwich cookies and place the crumbs in a zip-top bag. A grandparent makes up one package of instant chocolate pudding while grandkids shovel one table-spoon of cookie crumbs into clear plastic cups. Into the pudding that's been cooled for five minutes, stir in one tub of Cool Whip and half of the cookie crumbs. Fill the cups three-quarters full with pudding mixture and top with remaining crumbs. Refrigerate for an hour and top with gummy worms and frogs. Then let the grandchildren dig into the dirt!

Bake your name and make bear families. Use a can of refrigerator breadstick dough to let your grandchildren form their names on a cookie sheet. Brush with melted butter or a beaten egg and add cinnamon sugar for an extra treat. Bake for 15 minutes at 350 degrees. You can also use the bread dough to make bear families with a bear to represent each person in the family.

Jelly bean picture. This recipe is for kids older than three, since jelly beans can be choking hazards. Cover a piece of cardboard with aluminum foil, and spread white frosting all over the foil. To make a picture, let the kids put the jellybeans wherever they like. Later they can eat or just display. You can adapt this activity to Christmas by using red and green jelly beans; Fourth of July with red, white, and blue jelly beans for flags and fireworks; or Easter with pastel jellybeans.

Cookie-Baking Tradition

My childhood friend Mary Mayer has a cookie-baking tradition. Because her grandboys are young and have short attention spans, they make simple treats: mini chocolate pretzels, pre-cut-out sugar cookies, and reindeer cookies—their favorites. This year Nana and PaPa bought red children's aprons for each grandson, and fun airplane-shaped and race car spatulas; these stay at the grandparents' house for the next baking time. Afterward, they sample the treats and make samplers on small paper plates to send home or give to neighbors.

When you make a tradition of having certain foods every time your grandchildren come to visit, and they get to help in the preparation, it forms a memory for both of you. And whether it's making blueberry muffins or chatting while you sit around the kitchen island snapping green beans, you make great connections with your grandsons and granddaughters. You may even be the catalyst for your grandchild's budding career as a chef!

Even if you're far away, you can still interact in the kitchen. Mix up your best chocolate chip cookies in front of a video camera as if you were on a cooking show. Dress up and use a funny voice to make your grandkids laugh. Then mail your grandchildren a package of the cookies, the video, and the recipe. Even without a video or DVD, cookies from grandparents are always a special treat from across the miles.

My five-year-old grandson Ethan

and I bake cornbread almost every time we're together. It started a couple of years ago when he was visiting and helped me fix cornbread for the dinner one evening. That's all it took. Ethan was a picky eater, but he wanted some of what he had cooked. Now every time we're together, he asks for us to bake cornbread. He helps me in the kitchen with other cooking, but cornbread is "our thing." It will be a wonderful memory for us both.

—Becky McCormick

My grandmother Helen was the most wonderful baker. When I was a child she would have me over and we'd spend the day in the kitchen baking. I'll never forget all the wonderful things we made together: pancakes and pies, layer cakes, and strawberry bread. Now I make some of those delicious foods for others and teach my grandkids how to make them. But no one can match my grandmother's baking skills!

—Elizabeth Wickland

Mary's Super-Easy Treats for Holidays

Mini chocolate pretzels. Line a cookie sheet with foil. Kids place miniature pretzels on cookie sheets and put a Rolo candy in the center of each one. Bake at 300 degrees for just a few minutes to soften the chocolate candy. Put a small pecan half in the center of each Rolo and press down till it spreads across the top of the pretzel; Grandparent, do this so your grandchild doesn't get burned—the chocolate will be hot. Let cool on wax paper, then remove. Even very small children can make these and enjoy.

Pre-cut-out sugar cookies. Buy tree, pumpkin, or bunny-shaped sugar cookies from the refrigerated section at the grocery store. Let kids put a red hot candy at the top and decorate with sprinkles before or after baking. These are quick and easy, and the little ones have just as much fun as they would with old-fashioned, made-from-scratch cutout cookies.

Reindeer cookies. Buy a can of white or chocolate frosting, a bag of Oreo cookies, and a bag of mini pretzels. Together frost the top of the Oreos. Let the kids decorate to make a reindeer face: add a red hot for the nose and mini- or regular-sized M&Ms for the eyes. Break a mini pretzel in half and place two on top of the face for the reindeer antlers. Sometimes the faces almost look like alien creatures, depending on the colors the kids choose for eyes and where they put the eyes and nose. But these treats are lots of fun. Be sure to take pictures and look at them each year as the grandchildren grow.

Mini Easter cupcakes. Buy a white cake mix and canned frosting. Prepare the cake mix according to box instructions. Divide the cake batter into four to five bowls. Add a drop of food coloring to each bowl to make different batter colors: pink, pastel green, blue, and yellow. Leave one bowl of frosting white. Then drop batter into mini paper cupcake liners in the pan. After baking, decorate with frosting, coconut, and jelly beans. Grandkids will have fun making and decorating the cupcakes, then taking them home or sharing with others.

My foster daughter has two girls, six and eight; they call me Grandma Bonnie. We do a variety of activities when we're together, including shopping, rummage sales, and going to festivals, ball games, and to church. But their favorite bonding activity is working with me in the kitchen. They like making toast, scrambled eggs, mixing up a recipe, cutting up apples and cheese, practicing measuring, washing dishes, and playing in the water. Although it requires me to clean up when they're done, it's rewarding to see them enjoy serving others when our food is ready.
—Bonnie Kruizenga

> I like cooking because Mamo let me help her in the kitchen when I was only four. I got to stand on a chair and basically do a lot of the mixing and pouring. We made blueberry muffins for tea parties and Mamo set the table with her best china. Last year I got my first rolling pin and pumpkin pie is my specialty. Now I like to make quiches and chili and invite my grandmas over for lunch.
>
> —Caitlin, 10

Tips for Cooking with Grandchildren

When you mix enthusiastic, energetic children with flour, sugar, butter, and eggs, it can result in a lot of fun—and a big mess in your previously clean kitchen. That's why when you're cooking, you need some preplanning and lots of patience to enjoy the process and make a memory. Here are some tips to help with your "grandcooking" adventures.

Keep it simple and keep it fun. As Phyllis Stanley, a terrific bread baker who cooks with her grandchildren, always says, "Cooking is more of an art than a science. Turn mistakes into a new recipe!"

Allow enough time so you aren't rushed. If a recipe normally takes 30 minutes, double the time. Kids like to smell, taste, and touch. When you aren't on a deadline, the cooking session is more enjoyable and kids can stir and learn at their own pace.

Get a recipe box and recipe cards or make a small recipe book. Write down your specialty recipes, foods you make together, and family favorites. When your grandkids get home, you can exchange recipes by e-mail.

Don't sweat the small stuff. Purpose before you start not to worry about the mess that kids can create in the kitchen! Then you won't be disappointed or irritated with spilled milk and sticky counters. Savor the moments together and clean up later.

Get all the measuring cups and ingredients ready ahead of time, along with your mixer, spoons, and anything else you'll need for the recipe.

Try your favorites. Next time the kiddos visit, let them help you make your signature soup or favorite dessert. Invite them to assist in dinner preparation. With a little help, children can make a simple pasta meal with penne pasta and a jar of good Italian sauce, make hamburger into patties for a cook-out, cut up vegetables for salad, and lots more.

> **Cooking with your grandchildren**
> is a wonderful way to bond. You're focused on an activity, teaching life skills, and helping your grandchild feel recognized and valued. There's a shared sense of accomplishment in that.
>
> —Donna Butts

Chapter 13

Connecting through Storytelling

Storytelling is an act of devotion.
When we tell a story with enthusiasm,
we send children a clear message:
I care so much for you that I want to give you
the most precious gift I have—my time.
During those moments together,
nothing but the story matters.

—Charles A. Smith

Many children fall asleep with the TV on or plugged in to their iPods, after having spent hours playing computer games and watching movies. That's all the more reason to connect heart to heart with our grandkids through storytelling. Just look at the ways sharing simple stories can bless your grandkids. You can pass on enduring values through stories. Storytelling does lots of great things for their learning abilities: it instills good listening habits needed for school success; it develops concentration and a longer attention span; it helps kids understand sequencing, builds language comprehension, and expands their vocabulary. Their teachers will thank you!

Most of all, storytelling is just pleasurable. Reading a book aloud is wonderful. But hearing a story that requires your grandkids to make up pictures and scenes in their minds gives their imaginations a chance to grow. And it doesn't cost a dime. As grandparents, we can keep storytelling alive with just a little creativity—and not just at bedtime! You can tell your grandkids stories anytime you're together, even while you drive them somewhere in the car. You can tell them fantasy stories, personal stories from your own life, Bible stories, and even silly stories. Here's an example of how one grandma did this and how the tradition grew.

The Hibernating Bears Story and Game

Cynthia looked forward to visiting her three grandchildren in Bedford, England. But since she lived in Oklahoma and they saw each other only a few times a year, it usually took some time for the children to warm up to her. One day when she was trying to snuggle with four-year-old Kiah after reading to her at naptime, Kiah was rather standoffish and not at all interested in snuggling. Suddenly, Cynthia thought of an idea.

"Honey, come here," she said. "Let's play a little game called 'Hibernating Bears.'"

"How do we play that?" Kiah asked, her interest piqued.

"Well, you've got to get in the cave (the comforter on the bed they were sitting on) with Momma Bear."

"Who's the Momma Bear?"

"I am, and you can be the Baby Bear," Cynthia explained, "and we've got to get close to stay warm during the winter. That's how we bears hibernate. We take a long winter's nap."

Kiah scampered under the covers and snuggled close to her grandma, waiting for what came next. In a moment or two she started wiggling and asked, "When do the hibernating bears get to come out and play?"

"I'll go outside now and see if it's spring yet. You stay here and keep warm." As Cynthia peeked out of the comforter, she said, "It's not spring yet. It's still icy and snowy out there so we'd better stay in the cave."

Before getting back under the covers, she scratched on the blanket and said, "Somebody's knocking on our door. I think it's a lady. Should I open it?"

Kiah answered yes, so her grandma said, "You stay here and be safe while I go to the door and see what the visitor wants."

"What do you want in the middle of winter?" she asked the lady.

In a slightly scary voice, Cynthia, pretending to be "the lady," answered, "What do you mean? It's May."

"How can it be May? It's still cold and snowy outside. We're bears and we're hibernating," said Cynthia in her normal voice.

"Well, I like winter; I only like cold things, so I made it winter all year long. In fact, I'd melt if it wasn't winter," said the lady in a harsh voice.

"My cub needs food and if we can't have spring, there won't be anything for us to eat," Momma Bear answered.

"Oh, you have a cub? I like fur coats! I'd like to meet your cub!"

"I'll have to talk to my little cub about that," Momma Bear said.

She went back under the covers and asked Kiah if she wanted to meet the lady. "But let's think of a plan first, just in case," she suggested.

Together Momma and Baby Bear came up with two possible solutions:

Since the lady only liked cold, they could invite her in for tea and spill hot tea on her so she'd melt and it would become spring; or, they could give her tea and sweets, pretending all the time it's sour candy, and that would make her melt.

"Which do you choose?" Momma Bear asked.

Kiah decided on the "sweet" solution, so that was how the story went. Poof! After a taste of the sweet candy, the lady melted and it turned into spring. Then it was time for some outdoor fun for the bears; Kiah came up with searching for honey. Like all kids, Kiah is good at pretending and adding her own parts to the story. The search for bees and honey resulted in Baby Bear falling out of a tree, so they ran to the human hospital. Later, they hunted for berries and made a blackberry pie. They went to the river and fished for their dinner. When Momma Bear got tired, they got under the covers to hibernate for another winter; before long, Kiah fell asleep.

This storytelling adventure not only helped Cynthia connect with her grandchildren in England; when other grandkids in Oklahoma City and St. Louis heard about Hibernating Bears, they wanted to hear and act out the story themselves!

Now they all create their own version of the Hibernating Bears' adventures when their grandma comes to town. It's a great connecting activity. Caleb wanted a dragon in the tale, so the dragon comes to the door instead of the cruel lady. They go on a bear hunt and growl through the forest. They visit some campers and are surprised that saying, "Good morning!" in bear language—a big growl—makes the humans run away and leave their food behind for the bears. Each grandchild has added his or her own spin to the story.

Cynthia doesn't consider herself especially creative, but she finds if she just starts something fun—a story or a pretend game—creative ideas will follow. She adapts little ideas from other stories that come to her mind, such as The Three Bears or the Narnia tales; with the grandkids' creativity, the story continues to expand. They never run out of ideas for the adventures of the Hibernating Bears.

Davy Crockett and Other Tales for Grandkids

Our three grandsons, Caleb (seven), Noah (six), and Luke (five), love Davy Crockett stories. I read them a few books from the library about the frontiersman's adventures, but they wanted more. I found that when they spend the night, the best way to get them relaxed is to have them get under the covers, turn out the lights, lie beside them, and make up more Davy Crockett stories. One time a snake bit Davy as he was fording a river, and once he wrestled a crocodile in a swamp. One night the boys wanted to hear how Davy and Jim Bowie, of Bowie Knife fame, became hunting buddies when they were kids. Before long, the grandboys were fast asleep and I could rest from our busy evening of play.

> Grandparents are as cozy
> as a comforter.
> They add an extra
> layer of love.
> —Unknown

Now, I've never considered myself a natural-born story-teller. Not like my imaginative brother George, who told stories of Cowboy Bob to his sons and will share them with his grand-kids when they come along. He got the idea for the Cowboy Bob stories from a painting of a cowboy on horseback herding cattle across a wide prairie. In the stories George spins, Cowboy Bob rides his famous horse Paint across the plains, is chased by wild bush dogs, and leaps across canyons. George always put his sons in the story, which added great interest. "Cowboy Bob rode by a newcomer's ranch and saw Jon and Zack. He asked them to go along fishing with him and they caught the world's biggest fish."

> Grandchildren bring sunshine into my heart
> And laughter into my household.
> Their visits may be long or short, but always memorable.
> I tell them my stories and they tell me theirs right back.
> It's my grandchildren that actually made me
> a grandparent,
> So I'm eternally grateful.
> They always bring such spirited joy into my life.
> —Anonymous

From listening to Oklahoma taletellers at festivals, I learned to start the story and then let my grandkids participate by completing the action or a part of the plot. Here's an example: "Suddenly Davy Crockett came upon a…" I stop and ask Noah or Luke what Davy encountered and what he did next. This active involvement in the story holds children's attention and builds their creativity, imagination, and storytelling skills.

Here are some great suggestions for story starters.

Use familiar storylines. Children love repetitive themes and characters like the Hibernating Bears or the Davy Crockett stories. Create your own signature story by starting with a character you make up, like The Mysterious Horse or Sandy the Dog. Whenever you're together, share a new episode of his or her adventures.

Put your grandchild into the story. For example, I might say, "When Davy and Jim Bowie got to the fort, they found Noah and Luke sitting by a fire cooking dinner. They were so hungry from scouting for the cavalry that they asked the boys if they could join them. Later that night all four of them went on an adventure in the woods."

To make Bible stories even more engaging, put the child in the story or parable. Your granddaughter could be Queen Esther's best friend. Your grandson could be the boy who brought the donkey for Jesus to ride into Jerusalem. By doing this, you'll be personalizing the story and conveying truth at the same time.

> Where do stories come from, does anybody know? Where do stories come from, and where do stories go? Stories come from deep inside, then they travel far and wide.
> —Unknown

Take a character from a favorite children's book and make up more stories about this character's adventures. If Thumbelina is your granddaughter's favorite character, let her be your springboard. If The Three Billy Goats Gruff is a favorite, create interest by using a different voice for each billy goat and the troll.

Round-robin tales are fun story-starters and a great way to involve grandpa and additional grandchildren who are visiting. One person begins the tale, the next person in the circle adds some more action and perhaps a new character, then the story line passes to the next participant.

Tell stories about their parents. Kids love to hear stories about what their moms and dads did when they were young. They especially enjoy "scar stories," about when parents got their first black eye or went to the hospital for stitches.

Save your old hats or collect them from garage sales and thrift shops. Hats stimulate dramatic play and serve as great story-starters, both for you and your grandchildren.

Learning to Tell a Tale ✳

If storytelling is new for you, a great place to start is to learn the plot of a children's book and tell the story, instead of reading it, to your grandchild. Here are some helpful tips.

✳ Choose a story that was a favorite of yours from childhood, such as Goldilocks and the Three Bears, or Hansel and Gretel. Or, pick a book your grandchild loves. Read the story over several times.

✳ As you read, you'll begin to get an idea of the basic text. You don't need to memorize the entire narrative. Just jot down an outline of the main events of the plot in sequence, noting the main characters and the important words. Review this outline mentally.

✦ Picture the story by scenes. This didn't come naturally to me since I don't have a great visual memory, but it's good exercise for our brains and really works to cement the story in our minds. Give it a try!

✦ Practice telling the story in your own words to the mirror or even to your pet.

✦ If you need extra practice, record the story on CD and use it to rehearse in the car while you're running errands. After telling the story, give the CD to your grandchild to take home.

✦ When you tell the story, add your own gestures, dialect, repeated phrases, and props—even a musical instrument—as you'd like. Make the story original by using your own style.

✦ Relax, let yourself go, and enjoy the story. Your grandchildren will be mesmerized by the fun of tale-telling; they'll want to tell you a story in return.

> **When my grandchildren were younger,** ages three to nine, they loved listening to recordings their great-grandfather had made for them of his adventures as a boy with his next door neighbor, Timmy. My dad apparently spent many hours on space journeys, exploring jungles, and living with penguins at the South Pole. He told these stories with much enthusiasm to me when I was a child, to our children, and now to their children, through cassette tapes. They love to lie in their beds with the lights out and listen to "Great PaPa" talk about his travels. And we love that they are hearing him with his own voice now, several years since his death at age 94.
>
> —Diane Lister

Podcasting Your Stories: Grandparents Go Live!

Take heart if you don't have the opportunity for many in-person storytelling times. Even long-distance grandparents can give the gift of tale-telling. Prepare the story as discussed in the section above, and tell it via webcam. If it's a young grand-daughter and you have a puppet around the house, let the puppet tell the story and she'll be enchanted. Chapter 9 gives more information and ideas about using the webcam for video conversations and storytelling.

When the grandchildren are a hundred miles away, you can still tell an engaging story about your mischievous dog or share the adventures of Sinbad the Sailor by podcasting your stories. Podcasting is an Internet technology that allows you to record and post audio to broadcast your voice, not to just one grandchild, but all of them at the same time, no matter where they live—even on the other side of the world.

There are different programs that support podcasting such as Audacity (a free program) and Windows Sound Recorder. Search out the one that's most user-friendly and cost-effective. All you need is a computer and microphone, but if you have a webcam, either built-in or portable, that will work.

You'll also need a site to host your podcast; there are free ones such as podbean.com or onstreammedia.com. All the different programs have detailed directions on how to produce and distribute your podcast.

As a less techy alternative to podcasting, you can make an audio recording on a CD or a video of yourself telling stories, then send the recording to your grandchild as a birthday or Christmas gift. They'll love hearing you tell a story and, if it's on video, seeing you as well. One of children's favorite topics to hear about is their family history.

Family History Stories

Once during a family reunion in Kansas, my husband Holmes, our children, and I sat around Uncle John as he related a favorite Fuller family story, John Matthias Goes to Dodge City. Kids and adults listened with wide eyes and attentive ears as Uncle John told tales of the Old West, such as this one.

My dad, John Matthias Fuller, went to Dodge City, Kansas, as a young man before the railroad lines were built, because Dodge was having a boom—lots of jobs, money, and opportunity. John was a city slicker but decided that since all the cowboys out there were wearing guns, and he wanted to be in style, he'd go and buy a big six-shooter, belt, and holster. He was a peaceful man who'd never hurt anyone, but he wanted to fit in.

One Sunday morning, John decided to try his gun out and sneaked down the street wearing his big, shiny six-shooter. Suddenly someone grabbed him by the collar and said, "Hand me that gun and gun belt!" That was Bat Masterson, the famous marshall of Dodge City. "Young man, you don't wear a gun in this man's town. You'll just be fodder for the guys who know how to use one. I'm going to take this gun and gun belt and keep them in my office until you leave. Then you can take them with you."

> Grandparents are living links to the past, even as they encourage their grandchildren to dream of the future.
>
> —Archie Dunham

John stayed there in Dodge City three months, and then decided to go back to Kansas City to work for his older brother. The last thing he did was go and get his gun. There was a clerk in the marshall's office who said, "What will you take for that gun?" The clerk had a roll of bills, so John sold the gun to him. In the end, Dad didn't wear a gun very long, but he did go to Kansas City a few dollars richer!

Throughout the afternoon, Uncle John spun stories of the

Fuller brothers staking a claim on the Cherokee Strip and told how John Matthias began his building career. We all loved the story of Grandma Fuller and Her Knitting Needles. During World War I all the townspeople brought her yarn and she knitted woolen hose and gloves for the soldier boys in France. How those steel knitting needles would fly while she read her big Bible propped up in front of her!

We all have a story to tell. Each family has a rich store-house of tales: stories of faith and overcoming adversity, stories of ancestors immigrating to the U.S., stories that show how God redeems the mistakes of ordinary people, and stories from different periods in our nation's history. A family history story is a love gift from parent to child, then grandparent to grandchild. It conveys a sense of family belonging, connecting the child to the past, and giving him confidence to go on into an uncertain future. As children discover who they are and where they came from, their sense of identity grows. Family stories provide a bridge for sharing life and building relationships.

Whether these stories are told around the dinner table when grandkids visit us, during a family reunion, or even in a letter, storytelling provides a way to pass on important life messages and create family memories.

Family History Letters

When Cindy's daughter was pregnant, Cindy and her daughters were looking at their baby books and found letters written by Cindy's mom, who was in heaven. Seeing how much those letters meant to her daughter, Cindy decided she would write letters to her own little granddaughter. Before long, this idea grew into quite a project. Cindy had lost her mother, father, and mother-in-law in the three years before little Katherine was born; she would lose her brother shortly after giving birth.

Sad that her grandchildren would never know these dear ones, Cindy decided to write a letter to Katherine every month and introduce her to one of her family members who had gone home to heaven. She included pictures of the family members at different stages of their lives.

Here is how she made this new family tradition. On the day Katherine turned one month old, Cindy wrote a handwritten letter on her best stationery, telling the baby how much she loved her and how amazing her birth and first month had been. The following months, she printed the biography letters on computer stationery.

The beginning of each letter is a personal note to the child about special things she's done that month, milestones reached, and holidays celebrated. Then Cindy introduces the family member her granddaughter will meet in the letter. She gives the person's full name, and date and place of birth; if they have passed away, she adds the date and place of death. Then she shares all she can remember about that person. It's a little history lesson as Cindy mentions service during wars, tells of what life was like before computers or television, and describes that family member's interests.

The first biography letter was about Katherine's mom, then her dad, then Grandma (Cindy) and Grandpa, their aunts, parents, and great uncles and aunts. Though it was time-consuming, Cindy enjoyed this walk down memory lane and her children looked forward to receiving the letters to see who would be featured next.

She saved the letters on her computer along with the pictures, so when the second grandbaby came along, she just had to personalize the letters for Sophia. Cindy is saving these biography letters in scrapbooks named Letters from Nana, and hopes they will be enjoyed by the children when they're old enough to read them.

Priming the Pump

Getting out a family tree and looking at old photo albums often primes the story pump. Children love to look at baby

How to Generate a Family History Story

There is an African saying, "When an old man dies, a library burns to the ground." Don't let your storehouse of stories burn down! Instead, start passing them on by asking yourself or a family member questions such as these. This set of questions begins by asking about an older relative's childhood home.

1. Can you picture your childhood home? Try to picture it just as it was, in detail, or even draw a simple house plan including the yard, the tree you played under, the house, the fireplace, and the dinner table where your family gathered. Think about events that happened there.

2. Who were the people who lived there with you? What were they like? Did you all get along well?

3. What visitors came most frequently? Include relatives, friends, and extended family.

4. What kind of neighborhood was the house or apartment located in? How did you feel about it?

5. What was going on in the world at the time you lived there? Who was President of the United States? Was the nation at peace or at war? What was the economic and social climate like? Which movies, songs, and radio and television programs were popular? Who were your favorite entertainers? What were the fashions like?

Thinking about these things generates great family stories!

pictures of themselves, siblings, and parents, as well as photos of relatives. They are often fascinated by the stories and history that surround these family images. Share information like this.

✮ "This picture of Aunt Earlene was taken in 1935 in Hollywood, where she worked as a double for Dorothy Lamour in a Bob Hope movie."

✮ "This picture of Grandma and Granddad was made when he came back from the war."

✮ "This is a picture of your father and me on our honeymoon in Niagara Falls."

When a photo or memory primes the pump and you want to tell a true story from your own experience, these guidelines will help.

✮ Remember a specific age—when you were eight years old, or had just graduated from high school.

✮ Tell about the time during that period when you were happiest, saddest, or most fearful.

✮ Relate the dialogue. What would you have said and what did others say to you?

✮ Recall the sights, smells, tastes, sounds, and feelings of the experience.

✮ Share some special insight you gained from that experience.

Drawing Closer through Storytelling

Whether you spin a fantasy tale or share family history stories with your grandchildren in person or by long distance, storytelling is a great way to establish communication and closer contact. If your grandchildren aren't interested in hearing the stories now, keep a journal and save them for later. Record an audio or video gift of you sharing not only your family's history, but also your own life stories.

In whatever form it takes, storytelling helps relieve everybody's stress at the end of the day. It can even come in handy on a trip when the grandkids have already asked several times, "When will we be there?" Stir up your creativity and have fun making up stories and remembering personal histories that entertain and delight.

And remember, anytime you sit down and tell a story—even if it's on the Internet—you're creating a valuable moment together, time you'll never regret investing in your grandchild.

Grandchildren invest in our lives, too. Spending time with them is life's best preventative medicine. It can give you a new lease on life!

> **You are their link with the past.**
> Tell them of struggles overcome, heroes in the family history. Grandparents impart history and values by their very existence; it made the existence of their grandchildren possible.
>
> —Robert Aldrich, M.D. and Glenn Austin, M.D.

Chapter 14

Encouraging Your Grandchildren's Reading

If you see a book, a rocking chair, and
a grandchild in the same room,
don't pass up a chance to read aloud.
Instill in your grandchildren a love of reading.
It's one of the greatest gifts you can give.

—Barbara Bush

What a privilege it is to read to our grandchildren and share our love of books! I remember what fun it was to read to our first grandkids, Caitlin and Caleb, books like *Goodnight Moon*, the Richard Scarry books that were their dad's favorites as a toddler, *The Tales of Peter Rabbit*, and *Corduroy*, the story of a little brown bear that wanted a home. It's been a pleasure to read to my other grandchildren when I'm in their homes or when they come to visit. They love books like *Paddington Bear*, *The Real Mother Goose*, *Winnie the Pooh*, and *The Little Engine That Could*. One of our favorites is *The Three Billy Goats Gruff*, which we read with different voices for the troll, the baby goat, and his brothers.

A wonderful part of being a grandparent is contributing to our grandchildren's education; there's no better way to do that than encouraging them to read. Kids learn to enjoy reading when the adults around them love reading. Helping them become avid readers doesn't take a large bank account; we don't even have to be there in the same room! As Barbara Bush said, it's one of the best gifts we can give.

As we encourage their reading, we are helping our grandchildren be more successful in every subject. It's the most important of all academic skills because almost 90 percent of all schoolwork requires reading—even math! Reading develops kids' imagination, grammar abilities, and especially their listening and communication skills.

Research shows that a child who listens well as a result of being read to by the adults in her life, is able to retell stories and repeat instructions better at a young age. Children who are good listeners in kindergarten and first grade tend to become successful readers by the third grade. Fifth-graders with good listening and language skills are likely to do well in aptitude and achievement tests in high school. Whatever age your grandchildren are, encouraging their reading today will bring benefits for many years to come. Besides, reading is one of the joys in life and a great vehicle for connecting with them!

When we read to a child it helps him feel wanted and loved. It gives him an awareness of the world around him and builds up a background of experiences. Someone once said, "If you touch the heart with one book, it can transform a life." I believe it can.

Instilling a Love of Reading

Kids today are immersed in technology—television, movies, video games, computers—yet are often reading-deprived, lacking the time in their very busy homes to curl up with a good book. Fortunately there are lots of simple, creative, inexpensive ways we can instill a love of reading. As someone once said, the best thing you can do to raise a lifelong reader is to grab some well-chosen books and crack a smile. Don't forget to smile as you try some of these reading-stimulators!

Make a library visit. When grandkids come to your home, make it a tradition to head for the library soon after their arrival. Public libraries have not only books, but also audio books, music CDs (great for playing in the car as you drive somewhere), educational games, movies, and much more. Spend time looking at books with your grandkids and letting them pick out their very favorites. Some may choose nothing but sports hero books. Your granddaughter may want books about ballet and gymnastics. Other kids want to read about World War II weapons and tanks, books on oceanography and marine life, or fashion and style. Bring a canvas bag and let grandkids load it up with books to read at bedtime. Or, just give them time to peruse picture books between the activities you've planned. When you get home, put the books in accessible places and make it a point to turn off the TV.

We can encourage the reluctant reader by letting him watch a movie, such as *Black Beauty*, before he (or we together) reads the story in book form. When a group of children watched programs such as *George Washington, Raising the Titanic*, or a National Geographic special, all the books on those subjects quickly disappeared from the school library. Since they are a visual generation, seeing a video first can stimulate their interest in reading more about the topic.

Capitalize on their individual interests. Every child has what's called a "center of learning excitement," a subject that fascinates them, about which they'd like to know more. If you can tap into this center, whether it's science fiction or space exploration, motorcycle maintenance or making money, you'll go a long way in sparking her reading. And don't forget to take a bag of books along when you travel with your grandkids!

Glue fascinating or humorous illustrations from magazines or greeting cards in a notebook. During times you're together, invite preschoolers or those in early elementary school to dictate a story to go with one of the pictures. Save the stories in a folder for them to read when they are older.

Collect seasonal books and make books part of your holiday traditions. When our children and their spouses and grandkids come visit for Christmas, Thanksgiving, Easter, or another holiday, it's an ideal time to read them a book. I started collecting Christmas books when my children were young. During the month of December, I put a big basket full of these holiday treasures by the fireplace or Christmas tree: *A Cup of Christmas Tea, The Littlest Angel, The Other Wise Man, The Nativity*, and many others, including Christmas board books for babies and toddlers. It's a joy to get these books out and read to my grandchildren. We don't get them all read in one holiday visit, but over the years we will enjoy quite a few together! Sometimes the grands plop down by the basket and read a book themselves, or read one to their younger cousins. I've collected several Easter books and books on Thanksgiving themes to share as well, and I always send a valentine book to my out-of-town grandkids in a surprise package that arrives on Valentine's Day.

Bedtime reading. When your grandchildren visit your home, make sure you provide a bedside light and a stack of books for their own quiet reading time before lights out. You may want to give kids an extra 15 or 20 minutes if they're reading, to encourage them to get hooked on books.

When you play board games that involve reading, such as Scrabble or Scrabble Junior, you not only see how they operate in the world of competition and games, but you encourage their language skills and give them opportunities for reading practice.

Help kids make their own books. One of the most powerful language activities for young children that helps the reading-writing connection (a crucial step in cognitive development) "click" in their brains is to have them tell you a story as you write it down. Then make a book out of it. You can do homemade book bindings with a hole punch and yarn or by stapling pieces of white typing paper together. Put one sentence on each page with the child's illustration. Once the story is in book form, read it back to the child.

Let's say that you have read Little Red Riding Hood or The Three Bears to your grandchild on several occasions and she wants to tell her own version of the story. While she tells you the story, act as her secretary and write it down. As you dictate, she learns that her ideas can be put down on paper with word symbols. She begins to understand what writing is, which sparks her interest in expressing herself on paper as well as reading the work of other authors.

Take them to a bookstore. When Marsha's grandkids spend the night at her home, one of their favorite outings is a trip to the local bookstore where they can drink lemonade in the children's area while looking at books together. It connects reading with "the fun factor." They love being read to and perusing the stacks of books because Grandma has been taking them to the bookstore since they were toddlers. When they took a one-day vacation and went "cave-exploring" in a state park near their area, they read a book on the subject the next time they went to the bookstore. And when they get to pick out a book to buy and add to their home library, it's a big day!

Buy books as gifts. Lots of toys we give our grandchildren may end up lost, broken, or in next summer's garage sale. But a good book, a children's story they come to treasure, lasts far beyond the latest gadget or electronic toy. When we give a book as a birthday present or for another occasion, we're sending children the message that books are valuable!

Maria Cayere of Fairfax, Virginia, loves to give books as gifts. Receiving these special books from Grandma has helped make her granddaughter Anna Maria, who lives in Japan, an avid reader. Her favorites are chapter books about fairies. There are so many collections: The Jewel Fairies collection; the Pet Fairies series; and the Days of the Week fairy books. When Maria finds a new fairy book, she calls Anna Maria to let her know she's mailed it. The little girl can't wait to get the package. There are many collections about fairies, so Anna Maria is always waiting for the mail to bring her the next fairy book.

I love to pick out a book a grandchild would be interested in, inscribe it with his or her name and the date, and include it with another present. Here's a sample inscription: "Happy 8th birthday, Caleb, from Nandy and Poppa, February 2008." Mark milestones with gift books, adding inscriptions to celebrate "firsts," graduations, awards, and birthdays. For example, when I was in Milwaukee right before Josephine was about to start kindergarten, I picked out a book on starting school at Barnes & Noble and inscribed it: "With love to Josephine on starting kindergarten! August, 2007."

Recording Books and Stories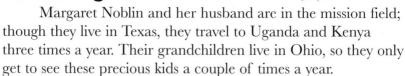

Margaret Noblin and her husband are in the mission field; though they live in Texas, they travel to Uganda and Kenya three times a year. Their grandchildren live in Ohio, so they only get to see these precious kids a couple of times a year.

Several years ago, Margaret made two books for their oldest grandson Stephen about his visits to Mema and Grandpa's house. One was about a visit to Turtle Creek to feed the ducks, something Margaret did as a small child with her grandparents. The other book was about Stephen's favorite car, Margaret's yellow VW Bug, which Stephen affectionately calls "the ladybug." Both of the books were memory makers for Stephen. Margaret's daughter said he loved to read them over and over and look at the photos of the activities they did together when he visited.

When Hannah and Samuel were added to the crew, Margaret began recording some of their favorite stories on CDs, so that even when she was in Africa, they could hear her voice read to them. Recently her daughter mentioned that the kids had gotten the CDs out and were playing them; even Peter, the youngest, listened attentively because he recognized Mema's voice.

One of the best things you can do to encourage reading as a long-distance grandparent is to audiotape yourself and your spouse reading favorite stories, just as Margaret did. Then send your tapes or CDs on to the grandchildren. To add a nice personal touch, make up a story about your pet or birds in your garden or something else you've shared with them.

When Shirley and Gabe made audio books for their grandchildren, they made up Lassie stories since they'd read a Lassie book the kids loved. They also told stories about "Flutter," the white butterfly that flies through their flower garden. Audio books or CDs connect your hearts across the miles and reassure the children of your love and care for them—even while you're encouraging their reading and language skills.

> There is no Frigate
> like a book
> To take us Lands away
> Nor any Coursers
> like a Page
> Of prancing Poetry—
> This Traverse may
> the poorest take
> Without oppress of toll—
> How frugal is the Chariot
> That bears the Human soul.
> —Emily Dickinson

One of Anne's fondest memories was reading to her grandsons at bedtime, although after a busy day together, she sometimes dozed off before they did. When she and her husband returned home to Ohio, she recorded some of the best stories they'd read together; she wanted her grandsons to remember her, and also to let them know as they listened that they weren't forgotten. They listened to the "Grandma Tapes" at bedtime and whenever they missed school because of illness. They played one story so often that they asked her to record it again.

When you read a story on CD, make the "ding" sound with a bell when it's time for the child to turn the page; then send the book with the recording in the mail. You can also make videos of yourself reading books, then send the recording and the book in the mail so your grandchild can read the book "along with you" whenever he wants some Grandma/Grandpa time. Make recordings of your favorite Bible stories and send the CD so your daughter or daughter-in-law can play them in the car. There's something about hearing the familiar voices of Grandma and Grandpa that is comforting and calming.

You can also make a keepsake recording by collaborating with two or more readers—yourself and Grandpa, aunts, or cousins—to record a dramatic reading of a favorite book. Vary characters' voices, create a few sound effects, and add a "ding" to let grandkids know when to turn the page. Sing your favorite songs on the recording as an extra gift. Kids love to hear grand-parents sing, even if it's a little off-key.

With the technology of webcams and voice-audio software, we can read a book to our grandchild "live" over the Internet. You can make a copy of a book, mail it to your grandchild, then read the book over the Internet after it arrives. If the parents have a big computer screen, you can hold the illustrations up to the webcam so they can see the illustrations as you read.

Grandparents Sharing Books

A terrific way to boost your grandchildren's reading at any age—and to build your connection—is to share books by reading them simultaneously. This is an especially effective way of con-necting with teenage grandkids, so try it! If your fifth-grader is reading *Charlotte's Web* by E. B. White in English class, get a copy of the book and read along. When you talk on the phone, by webcam, or in person on a future visit, you can discuss the book you're both reading. Parents and grandparents sharing books is a proven, research-based way of encouraging kids' reading skills.

A 13-year-old I talked to didn't like reading at all, but did enjoy science. As a child, he'd gaze at the sky and remark, "Look at that meteor!" or, "Look at the Big Dipper!" In school, he was getting Cs and Ds and not doing his homework, even though he was bright.

One day his teacher gave him a science fiction book called *Dune*, which told the story of people who lived on a desert planet. For the first time in a long while, he got excited about a book. His dad got a paperback copy of his own to read so they could discuss the story together. Their relationship began to improve as they shared opinions about the book. Eventually they read other books together. The teenager's attitude and grades improved along the way.

In the Author's World: A Book Club for Granddaughters

Phyllis Stanley wanted to encourage her granddaughters' reading skills, so she started a summer reading and writing club. One of the granddaughters was an avid reader and the other one wasn't quite as interested—but they both loved the club idea. Phyllis called it In the Author's World. She asked a 24-year-old friend to facilitate the club time for the girls. Every week the young woman comes and gives them "fun work"; they're learning about British authors and their works, such as A. A. Milne and Beatrix Potter. They're reading C. S. Lewis's *The Chronicles of Narnia*, Wordsworth poems, the Ryan Jakes series, and even a little Jane Austen thrown into the mix.

> It is a great thing to start life with a small number of really good books which are your very own.
>
> —Sir Arthur Conan Doyle

Grandma's not there when they discuss the books with their club leader, but she's helped design the whole course of reading. The girls are going to act out some of the stories after reading them, including three chapters of *The House at Pooh Corner*.

Phyllis gave each granddaughter a quote box to decorate and supplied them with white index cards to write down a favorite quote or two from every book they read. What a memory the girls will have as they look back on their summer in the author's world!

Reading by Example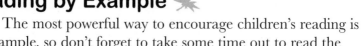

The most powerful way to encourage children's reading is by example, so don't forget to take some time out to read the newspaper, the comics, the Bible, or your current favorite fiction while the grandkids are around. Seeing your joy and laughter as you're reading has an impact. Reading together fosters closeness; time spent giving focused attention as you read to grandkids at bedtime produces benefits for the relationship, whatever their age.

> When grandparents read to us, they don't skip. They don't mind if we ask for the same story over again.
> —An eight-year-old

Reading aloud with older children is equally important. Besides meeting their personal needs, it helps them continue to enjoy books for entertainment, so they won't automatically associate reading with textbooks and tests. Try having a read-aloud time after dinner, or listen to recordings of classics. In the winter when dark comes early and the cold wind rages, grandkids snuggle up to the fireside in sleeping bags and listen to *Daniel Boone*, Laura Wilder's *Little House on the Prairie*, or C. S. Lewis's *Prince Caspian*.

During Cousin Camp, have a wind-down reading time when older cousins read to the younger ones. When you take the grandkids on a trip, take a book along. You'll never regret the investment of time spent together as you see their reading blossom each year.

Can't-Miss Treasures

I personally feel that some classic children's books are so worthwhile that our grandkids shouldn't miss them. Add your own favorites to the titles mentioned in this chapter. While it's only a beginning, these books will form a solid background for language development, comprehension, and a wide vocabulary.

Preschoolers

✴ *The Very Hungry Caterpillar* and other Eric Carle board books

✴ *Madeline* by Ludwig Bemelmans

✴ *Goodnight Moon* by Margaret Wise Brown

✴ *The Courage of Sarah Noble* by Alice Dalgliesh and Leonard Weisgard

✴ *The Bears on Hemlock Mountain* by Alice Dalgliesh and Helen Sewell

✴ *The Little Engine That Could* by Piper Watty

✴ *Mother Goose* by various illustrators

✴ *The Tales of Peter Rabbit* by Beatrix Potter

✴ *Caps for Sale* by Esphyr Slobodkina

✴ *A Child's Garden of Verses* by Robert Louis Stevenson

✴ *Make Way for Ducklings* by Robert McCloskey

Elementary

✴ *Peter Pan* by J. M. Barrie

✴ *The Wizard of Oz* by L. Frank Baum

✸ *Caddie Woodlawn* by Carol Ryrie Brink

✸ *Hans Brinker and the Silver Skates* by Mary
   Mapes Dodge

✸ *The Black Stallion* series by Walter Farley

✸ *Johnny Tremain* by Esther Forbes

✸ *Across Five Aprils* by Irene Hunt

✸ *A Wrinkle in Time* by Madeleine L'Engle

✸ *The Chronicles of Narnia* series by C. S. Lewis

✸ *Heroes of History and Christian Heroes: Then &
   Now* series (Order from YWAMpublishing.com)

Pre-teen and High School Years

✸ *Little Women, Little Men*, and *Jo's Boys* by Louisa
   May Alcott

✸ *Pride and Prejudice* by Jane Austen

✸ *The Hobbit, The Lord of the Rings* by J. R. R.
   Tolkien

✸ *Jane Eyre* by Charlotte Brontë

✸ *Wuthering Heights* by Emily Brontë

✸ *The Pilgrim's Progress* by John Bunyan

✸ *Alice in Wonderland* and *Through the Looking
   Glass* by Lewis Carroll

- *The Last of the Mohicans* by James F. Cooper

- *All Creatures Great and Small* by James Herriot

- *Space Trilogy* by C. S. Lewis

- *The Adventures of Huckleberry Finn* and *Tom Sawyer* by Mark Twain

- *The Yearling* by Marjorie Kinnan Rawlings

Chapter 15

Being a Spiritual Influence In Your Grandkids' Lives

We're not keeping this to ourselves,
we're passing it along to
the next generation—
God's fame and fortune,
the marvelous things he has done.
—Psalm 78:4, The Message

One of Peggy Powell's greatest joys is when her seven grandchildren gather at their retreat home in Colorado each summer. They do all kinds of interesting things, from discovering, by measuring it, that Noah's ark was 150 feet longer than a football field, to using river rocks to learn the books of the Bible.

Each year they come up with a new theme for the week's activities. Their morning Bible time begins with the "Hero of the Day." One of their grandchildren carries the flag as they place it in its post on the hill looking out on Pikes Peak. They study a Bible character of the week, such as David, Daniel, or Noah, and take time for the cousins to pray for each other. The "Hero of the Day," an honorary position that rotates daily so that each grandchild has a turn, sits on the small blessing stool with a rimmed cookie sheet. On the cookie sheet are traits written on index cards that the children might want to develop in their lives, such as patience, courage, and kindness. The hero passes the cookie sheet around to each cousin; they, in turn, choose an area for improvement. Then each one is prayed for by another cousin, which thrills Grandma.

"Lord, will You make Cooper courageous and brave for the rest of his life?"

"Dear God, I pray You'll build patience in Madison."

Whether you have your grandchildren with you for a short time or an extended time, and whether you do simple things or elaborate ones, you'll find many ways to be a positive influence in the spiritual lives of your grandchildren.One of the best ways to do this is to pray with your grandkids; this helps them know God and experience His love, rather than just knowing about Him. Think about it as "taking them praying," instead of "teaching them to pray." As a grandparent, you are well qualified to lead the way!

Here are a few ideas to help you get started.

Sing a prayer. When we were in Switzerland, some Swiss children whom we visited taught us a happy mealtime prayer to sing. At first they sang it in French, then in English, so we could sing along. We taught it to each of our grandkids at a very early age; it remains their favorite way to say grace before eating when the family gathers.

Say "Wow!" prayers. "Wow!" prayers are a good way to say thanks to God as we go through our day without being overly "religious"; they help our grandchildren develop a grateful attitude. As Rabbi Marc Gellman, author of *How Do You Spell God?* said, "Wow! prayers are the way we say, 'This thing I just saw or ate or felt is terrific and beautiful or awesome, and I'm saying this thank you prayer so you know that I know that you had something to do with this. Keep up the good work!'"

As grandparents, we aren't always rushed and frantic to get everything on our to-do list accomplished—at least not as rushed as their parents are—when we're spending time with the grandchildren. So we can stop and let them look at the doodle bug in the dirt or lightning bugs in our backyard and talk about what they see. We can slow down enough to notice all the "Wow!" stuff in the world around us and thank God for it.

> One of our traditions is to gather around an outdoor fire pit in our yard on Halloween night and share about the Lord's goodness through stories of what He has done in the last year. We began this about 10 years ago when my husband went on a mission trip to Argentina on Halloween; the grandchildren came over not to trick-or-treat, but to roast hot dogs and marshmallows. The desire was to worship the Lord that particular night. Added to this fun several years later was watching a movie, because their fun-loving uncle suggested we not watch a movie IN the house, but OUT of the house. Granddaddy sets up a TV, DVD player, and sound system, and we watch a fun, clean DVD. So here sits the Kirkpatrick clan gathered around an outdoor fire pit in the cool night air of autumn, watching a TV late into the night. The grandkids look forward to this each year.
>
> —C.J. and Hollis Kirkpatrick

Little Visits with God and Bedtime Devotionals

When our children were young, we read them a nightly devotional called *Little Visits with God*; it not only reached their minds, but touched their hearts. The short stories were full of warmth and love, drawn right out of life situations. The old book came apart at the seams, so I was delighted to find the

Golden Anniversary Edition of *Little Visits with God*. It's a book that for 50 years has been blessing children, but the messages and stories aren't out of date. Its truths are timeless and can help guide the next generation's journey.

Now when our grandchildren spend the night, before lights out we have our Little Visit with God time right along with reading books like the Heroes of History and Christian Heroes series books on Daniel Boone, John Adams, and missionary Gladys Aylward. Recently when Noah, our six-year-old grandson, spent the night, we were cuddled up in my bed. I read him *The Rainbow Fish* and then he chose the devotional, "God Counts Our Hairs," from *Little Visits with God*. It is based on Matthew 10:30: "Even the very hairs of your head are all numbered."

When we pray, we share our love for Jesus.
When we are with our grandchildren, we gently and intentionally bring God's Word and meaningful sharing into our times together, whether around the table, camping, or celebrating in the backyard. In the car, we may listen to a book on audio and then discuss it. We've read missionary autobiographies and Ivan books. When we take them individually on their eight-year-old-trip, we have morning quiet times and prayer together. Holiday times around the table are wonderful times of celebrating the real meaning of Christmas, Thanksgiving, Valentine's Day, St. Patrick's Day, etc. It takes time to prepare for spiritual times together, but is well worth the investment! We're taking four of the grandkids on a camping trip soon; I'm bringing the children's version of *Hinds' Feet on High Places* for us to read together.

—Phyllis and Paul Stanley, Navigators missionaries

Noah was amazed to hear that God knows exactly how many red hairs are on his head. We talked about how God even cares for the little sparrows and not one can fall without God knowing—and that He knows all about us and takes care of us. As Noah fell asleep I prayed quietly that he would always know how much God loves him, and that he'll trust God as he grows up.

Cynthia's grandson Tate always wants her to tell—not read—him Bible stories about David and Goliath, Daniel in the lion's den, and other Bible heroes. Whenever her grandchildren spend the night, she shares a devotional with them from a children's Bible or devotional book, believing that if parents and grandparents wait until children are old enough to understand all the concepts, they'll be too busy. A prime time to share God's truth and love is when they are young.

There are countless devotionals for teenagers, too. One Texas grandma I know bought her granddaughter a book for teens on her 12th birthday titled *The One Year Designer Genes Devo*, by Ann-Margret Hovsepian; she bought a copy for herself as well. Reading through the daily devotional together, though they live in different cities, proved to be a conversation stimulator. They phoned and e-mailed each other often about what they learned from certain readings.

Pray Around the World

If you have a spinning globe of the world, use it as a great hands-on way to pray with children. After a meal, pass it around the table to each person, little or big. Each one twirls the globe, and when it stops, notes what country her hand is on. If she is too young to read the name of the country, you can help her say the name. Then she prays for anything that comes to mind: "God bless all the Susans in China" (or nine-year-olds if she's nine) or, "Heal all the kids who are sick in China."

Ways to Be a Positive Spiritual Influence ✴

Be a good role model. The single most powerful impact you can have on your grandchildren is through your example. Our grandchildren are watching, and what we do shouts louder than what we say.

Tap into teachable moments. We've all heard of the value of taking advantage of "teachable moments"; when you're with your grandkids, the possibilities are endless. When you're outside together and hear the wind rustling the leaves, talk about how even the leaves praise God. Use the seasons and cycles of weather, animals at the zoo, and the variety of trees and flowers to discuss the God who created all things, and how His creation expresses His love and goodness. The miraculous is all around us if we take time to notice.

Give God the credit when your grandchild is astonished by something: the Big Dipper on a clear night, a cluster of monarch butterflies, fragrant honeysuckle in your garden, or waves crashing against the shore at a beach. Just slow down, look, listen, and give God the credit. "Isn't God good to make those stars?" "God made the honeysuckle for you to smell and enjoy. Isn't He good to give us little blessings like this to brighten our day?" When your granddaughter says, "Look at that furry green spotted caterpillar!" you can point her to the Maker of that wondrous creature. When you're exclaiming over how much your grandson has grown, or looking at photos from when he was little, you can remark, "Isn't it great how God made you? The Bible says you are wonderfully made. You're His original handiwork" (Psalm 139).

Collect memory makers. When you are with your grandchildren in the summer or on a vacation, photograph or collect interesting objects from nature such as colorful leaves, seashells, a bird feather, or flowers. Use them to make a gratitude booklet or poster thanking God for all your blessings and memories.

Make a life lessons booklet. You can write down in a journal a few of the lessons you've learned in life and specify the experiences that helped you learn those lessons. Write one lesson a month until the journal is full of the values and wisdom you want to pass on. When the book is complete, send it to your grandchild to use as he or she continues the journey of life. A good movie to inspire you before you embark on this project is *The Ultimate Gift.*

Mark their Bibles. Denise, a Kansas grandma, has nine grandchildren, ages nine months to eight years old. She keeps notes in her Bible when she feels led to pray a certain verse for a grandson or granddaughter. She puts their initials and the date by the verse and records the prayer in a file folder on her computer. When the grandchild is old enough to read, she gives him a Bible in which she has highlighted in different colored pencils all the verses she has prayed for him since his birth. On the dedication page, she writes something that connects with his interests. For example, when she gave Silas his Bible, she wrote:

> *I know how you love treasures. In this book are all God's treasures and promises, and even more than that, God is the treasure I hope and pray you find. Be a seeker of the greatest Treasure!*
> *Love, Grandma*

Rocks of remembrance. A lovely hands-on way to celebrate God's goodness is to get smooth stones from a river and put them in a big unbreakable bowl. Provide a permanent marker and let your grandkids write a few words on the stones that represent something that God has done in their lives. Periodically put the jar on the table and go through the rocks together, talking about each event: "God provided a job for

Dad," "Kate got well when she had pneumonia," etc.

Handwritten recipes for life. Joan Helm, a grandma from
Connecticut, wrote down all her favorite recipes on cards for
each of her granddaughters, and put a Bible verse on each
card. For Spiced Tea, she wrote Proverbs 3:5-6. On Baked
Cheese Sandwiches she wrote, "Jesus is wonderful!" On Ro-
maine Mandarin Salad she wrote, "They that wait on the Lord
shall renew their strength," from Isaiah 40:31. Although these
cards are wonderful to pass down, the underlying influence is
simply the way this grandmother and grandfather live their
lives and reflect God's love.

Taking Root 🍁

We never know what will "stick" and take root in our
grandchildren's lives, but all the seeds we plant are valuable. We
water them with our prayers and sometimes our tears, but God
is the One who causes growth and brings the harvest in His time.

I love what Fern Nichols, founder and president of Moms
In Touch International, told me about time she spends with her
granddaughter Mikaila and how their experiences illustrate
how even the little things a grandparent does make an impact.
Every Friday, Fern goes to her daughter Trisha's house and
cares for Mikaila while her mommy teaches second grade part
time. From the time Mikaila was a month old until she was two
and a half, Fern would sing "Amazing Grace" as she fed her
granddaughter a bottle. When Mikaila graduated from the bottle to the sippy cup, they would still go to the couch where Fern
would feed her and sing "Amazing Grace."

One morning, Fern called her daughter and Mikaila
answered. She excitedly said, "Hi Nana!" and then broke out
in song. You're right—she sang "Amazing Grace"—the whole
first verse! Fern and Trisha were in a puddle of emotions,
amazed that this little girl was hiding truth in her heart at such
a young age.

Another day, when Fern was playing baby dolls with her granddaughter, Mikaila suddenly snatched up her two baby dolls, took them to the wall, sat them down, and exclaimed with a "mommy" look, "Time Out!" After about 15 seconds, she picked up both the dolls, gave them a hug, and said, "Now, everything is going to be all right; it's okay." She proceeded to take them to the couch and, while rocking back and forth, fed them and sang "Amazing Grace" to her dollies.

> **As we remain compassionate and loving** toward our grandchildren, we can teach them to develop discernment and make right choices. But in order to earn the right to be heard, we may need to walk with them through some of their movies, music, video games, fashions, and fads. We need to replace the stigma of "old-fashioned grandpa" with "up-to-date, well-informed, savvy, wise, and discerning grandpa"…Our torches will illuminate our grandchildren's paths more brightly when we are, in their eyes, both timeless and timely grandparents.
> —Tim and Darcy Kimmel, *Extreme Grandparenting*

"As we're faithful and intentional about speaking and singing God's Word to our grandchildren, no matter how young they are," Fern says, "God uses it to mold a life."

Chapter 16

Connecting Heart to Heart: Praying for Your Grandkids

*Our prayers live on before God
and God's heart is set on them, and prayers
outlive the lives of those who uttered them;
they outlive a generation, outlive an age,
outlive a world.*
—E. M. Bounds

When our first grandchild was born, I was quickly ushered into an understanding of the importance of praying for our grandkids. Sweet Caitlin was born a month early with the umbilical cord wrapped around her neck and fluid in her lungs. Even after the doctor administered oxygen, she was in severe respiratory distress and was transported to a neonatal intensive care unit (NICU) at another hospital where she could receive a higher level of care.

The doctors called baby Caitlin "a fighter"; her courageous spirit struggled for life as the medical team labored. Even with a ventilator, an oscillator, blood transfusions, and medication, all we heard for 48 hours was, "Still critical…the next few days will tell…wait and see."

Instead of just waiting, we prayed! As both sets of grandparents, along with aunts and uncles, knelt in the NICU family room and prayed, I was reminded of two critically ill kids I knew of whose recovery even the doctors had attributed to a large network of prayer on their behalf. In that moment, God prompted me to call others far and wide to join our family in praying for Caitlin. I contacted churches, prayer chains, and prayer ministries like Moms In Touch International—a network of praying moms I was a part of—and they contacted others. Soon a huge prayer team stretched from Oklahoma to Florida, Colorado to California, and around the globe to a missionary kids' school in Germany and the Children's Prayer Network of Australia. They all joined their voices in prayer for our grand-daughter.

> Prayer is inviting Jesus into your grandchild's needs.
>
> —Cheri Fuller

From little voices and grown-up ones, in childlike prayers and mature ones, God heard Caitlin's name over and over, day after day. When doctors warned, "This isn't going well; this is what needs to happen in her lungs," we passed that request on to the intercessors. We asked for more prayer for the nighttime hours because she seemed to suffer set-backs during those hours. Finally, on Thursday night of the second week, baby Caitlin improved. In fact, her doctor told us that her X-ray on Friday morning looked as though it showed different lungs than the ones he had examined on Thursday. Prayers continued as she was transferred from the ventilator to an oxygen "space helmet" and began the difficult task of breathing on her own. After another week, her lungs had recovered enough for her to go home.

Caitlin is now an active, bright, and wonderful 10-year-old who has done competitive rock-climbing, plays tennis, and loves riding her bike. How thankful we are for her life! Through that medical crisis, we learned so much about the importance of covering our grandkids in prayer by giving God specific requests—and the power of praying for them in community with other caring people.

Perhaps your grandchild's struggle isn't physical like our granddaughter's, but he may face other challenges, such as learning problems, loneliness during a change in schools, or living through a painful divorce. There is never a time when they don't need their grandparents' prayers!

Praying for Pre-Born Grandchildren

You, too, can bless your grandkids with your prayers, beginning even before they take their first breath.

Janet Page, a San Antonio grandma, prayed for her grandchildren as they developed from conception through delivery. She went to Web sites such as mypregnancy.com and read about the development stages so she could pray specifically. For example, during the time the baby's heart was developing, she prayed: *Oh, Lord, my grandbaby's heart is now beating. Would You not make it to beat only for You? Will You give my grandchild a heart to serve You and others? Would You make this child's heart tender to Your Word and wholeheartedly devoted to You?*

During the weeks the brain and nervous system were developing, Janet prayed: *Abba, Father, my grandchild's nervous system is developing today. Please see to it that every neuron is healthy. Help my grandchild not to be nervous or touchy, but filled with Your peace.*

Bookstores have many books that track the development of a baby. There are good Web sites where you can follow the developmental growth each month of the pregnancy, then tailor your prayers to that stage. Check out babycenter.com; you put in the baby's due date and they send you weekly updates about the amazing progress of baby's development via e-mail. Also look into pregnancy.org, babyzone.com, and mayoclinic.com.

A Blanket of Prayer

Having loved being a mom, Maggie looked forward to being a grandmother someday. From the time her kids were babies, she had prayed for her grandchildren-to-be. But when her son Dave fell in love with a young woman and asked her to marry him, the young woman rejected his family. Finally Dave's fiancée made him choose between her and his family. For three years Dave had no connection with his parents and siblings. Maggie was heartbroken.

But one day when she was in prayer for her son and his wife, she somehow sensed they were going to have a baby. She wrote the news in her journal and began crocheting a special gift for her first grandchild, knowing she might not see him or her for a long time.

"My precious one," Maggie wrote, "in celebration of your arrival, I've made you a special gift called a prayer blanket. When you are covered with it, know that you are covered in your grandma's prayers. Each tiny stitch represents a prayer prayed for you." What followed were 10 prayers based on verses in the Bible that were blessings, including, "You are marvelously made by divine hands. I pray you will know how spe-

My grandmother had a bulletin board

on the wall next to the chair where she had her prayer time. On the board were photos of all 25 of us grandchildren and 15 great-grandchildren. When we saw the bulletin board, we knew that our grandma was praying for us every day. As I grew up, at every juncture where I could have veered off the right path, someone or something came along to steer me in the right direction. I know it was the prayers of my grandmother—not just in my life but in my entire family. My parents carried that same torch and are making a great spiritual impact on their children and grandchildren through their prayers.

—Pamela Helm

cial you are to God" (Psalm 139); and, "Like a ball of yarn that turns into a beautiful blanket, God has a beautiful plan for your life. I pray you will discover it" (Jeremiah 1:5).

After the baby was born, Maggie gave the prayer blanket to her daughter-in-law as a shower gift, along with the letter. Little by little, the situation began to change between Maggie and her son and daughter-in-law, and healing slowly came in their relationship. The first time Maggie was allowed to see her grandson, she snuggled him in the prayer blanket she'd so lovingly made, looked in his beautiful blue eyes, and said her first words to him: "Jesus loves you."

Maybe, like Maggie, you aren't able to see your grandchild right after he or she is born. No matter whether you are close or far away because of distance or strained relationships, you too can connect heart to heart by making a prayer blanket for your precious one and choosing verses that express the love in your heart.

Praying through the Developmental Stages of Your Grandchild's Life

When we understand the developmental goals of each stage of a child's life, we can pray specifically for him or her. Here is a helpful guide.

Infancy through toddlerhood. Pray that your grandchild will develop trust and a strong sense of security as he bonds with his parents and family. When you visit and rock and feed him, these prayers prayed quietly can bless the phase of childhood when emotional security and trust are supposed to develop.

Toddlerhood. In what experts call "the age of autonomy," pray that your grandchild will develop a healthy sense of independence. In the toddler years, kids begin to see themselves as distinct from others and develop a self-concept. It helps to remember this so you can react with patience as your two-year-old grandson's favorite word becomes, "No!"

Early childhood. In these years, pray specifically for your grandkids to develop a healthy curiosity, learn to play well with others, and have chances to explore and create without fear of failure.

School age. Ages seven to ten are called the "industry stage" of childhood. Ask God to help your grandkids discover their gifts and talents and to develop a sense of joy and satisfaction in using their developing skills so that they believe, "I can do this. I have something to contribute."

Teen years. Peers become more and more important during the pre-teen and adolescent years. Pray for your grandkids' friends to be a good influence and for your grandchildren to be a positive influence on them.

Special Prayer Ideas

Handprint prayers. When you and your grandkids are together, choose different colors of card stock, one for each child. Trace their hands on the card stock; when they ask why, explain that you will put your hand on their handprint as you pray for them each day. Write their names on the handprints, add a verse or quote that reminds you of each child, and put it in your Bible. You can carry the handprints with you when you travel; even if you're in another state or country, you'll be connecting heart to heart with your grandchildren and their Creator who loves them even more than you do! Over the years, as you see those handprints grow and grow, your prayers will bless their lives in ways you can't imagine.

Pray God's Word and use a prayer card as a reminder. I've been using *Pray!* magazine's prayer cards; my current favorite is "Scriptural Blessings to Pray for Your Children." For example, in February, I prayed, "Lead my grandchildren to trust in You and know You." In March, I prayed for intimacy with God: "Draw my grandkids face-to-face with You so they might taste Your goodness and long for more of You."

In April, I prayed for spiritual blessings: "Remind my grandchildren that You have adopted them in love and enable them to experience every spiritual blessing You've provided in Christ Jesus." These prayer cards cover a lot of bases: their friendships, their parents, comfort, hope, rest, and much more. Another good prayer card for grandparents is "Scriptural Prayers for the Next Generation" (see navpress.com or praymag.com).

A special day of prayer for each grandchild. Kathy, an Illinois grandma, also found it helpful to designate days of the week for each grandchild to make praying for them more doable. Monday was Rhiannon's day; she'd pray specifically for Rhiannon's needs at school and any challenges she was facing. Tuesday was Lacey's day; Wednesday was for Sabrina; Thursday was Joshua's day; Friday was designated to Madeleina; and Saturday was Savanah's prayer day. Periodically through the year she wrote them notes sharing what she had been praying for them. On each child's day of prayer she puts a photo of that child up in her kitchen window.

Calendar prayers. Maybe instead of seven grandkids, you have twelve or more. If the number of grandchildren outnumbers your days, divide them among the days of the month. Let each grandchild pick his or her day; it might be based on a birth date or another favorite day. Write each name on your calendar with any specific needs the grandkids have. Then you can put your heart into praying for one at a time instead of just saying, "Bless Carly" or, "Bless Charlie." One year you could think of all the character traits you hope your grandchildren will develop, such as courage, kindness, creativity, and faith. Then assign a character trait or virtue to each day of the month and pray for God to develop that trait in your grandchildren's lives.

Let them know you're praying. When Jay Jones, a little boy with Down syndrome and a heart condition, was ill, his grandmother sent him a little "Pass It On" card. On it was a picture of an angel and Psalm 91:11: "For he will command his angels concerning you to guard you in all your ways." She signed the back "Love and prayers, Grandmom." Months later, Jay still put the card under his pillow every night and stood it up on his bedside table every day as a tangible reminder of his grandmother's love and God's protection. Little things can mean a lot to a grandchild.

> **They [our grandkids] have things** they are excited about, worried or disappointed over, and hoping for. When we make it our aim to take these things that mean so much to them to the God to Whom they mean so much, they become closer to our hearts. We may not be on their minds as much as they are on ours, but God can use our prayers to bless them on our behalf.
>
> —Dr. Tim and Darcy Kimmel, *Extreme Grandparenting*

The Power of a Grandma's Prayers

One of my favorite true stories demonstrates how a grandmother's prayers can outlive her. It's the story of Dennis Jernigan's grandma and her impact on his life. Once when we were serving at a conference in Tulsa, Oklahoma, Dennis told me that when he was a little boy, he went every day to his grandma's house down the street to practice the piano because his parents didn't own one. He loved how she stood behind him, listening to each song and encouraging him. He was 12 years old when she died. As an adolescent and through his early twenties, Dennis became involved in the gay lifestyle and was filled with great turmoil and confusion.

But in his mid-twenties Dennis's life turned around; he began to lead worship in a small church in Oklahoma City. He eventually married and had nine children. One weekend he took his band back to his hometown of Boynton, Oklahoma, to lead a community worship service.

At the close of the evening, a little silver-haired lady came up to the piano and said, "Dennis, isn't it wonderful how your grandma's prayers have been answered?"

He had no idea what she was talking about and asked, "What prayers?"

"I was your grandmother's lifetime prayer partner, and she told me how she'd stand behind you as you practiced the piano at her home each day and pray that you'd be used mightily to lead people to God through music and worship." Dennis has been leading people of all ages and walks of life into worship in the U.S. and around the world for many years. As he does, the effects of his grandma's prayers touch not only his life, but the lives of countless others.

Blessing Your Grandkids through Praying Together

Peggy Powell has a prayer partner; every week for 15 years they've prayed for their grandchildren on the phone at 7:00 a.m. for 30 minutes. These are two very committed grandmas! They choose one scripture a week to pray for their combined 11 grandchildren, and include special needs as they're aware of them. As a result of joining their hearts and petitions, these two praying grandmas have seen God work in their grandchildren's lives over and over. If two grandmas praying together form a powerful team, imagine what a group of grandparents could do!

When Dorothy's husband retired and they moved away from their grandkids, she wondered what she would do with all that free time she was going to have. With a desire to pass on the heritage she'd received from her parents and grandparents, she began a Grandmas In Touch group in their new location, covering her seven grandkids and their schools in prayer. Soon other women joined her.

When her granddaughters, Amelia and Alicia, had to move across the country during their kindergarten and first-grade years, Dorothy was concerned about the transition. As she and the other grandmas prayed, exciting things happened for the girls; the welcome their teachers and classmates gave them at the new school smoothed their transition. Dorothy was so happy that she sent a lapel pin and thank-you note to the girls' teachers that stated, "You don't know it, but you're an answer to my prayers!"

> Expect resistance,
> but pray for miracles!
> —Corrie ten Boom

Nita Peck, a Texas grandmother, started a prayer group when her oldest grandson was in the second grade and prayed him all the way through college. Monday nights she would call her grandsons and say, "Tomorrow's my grandma's prayer group. What do you want me to pray for?" Sometimes it was a band tryout or a math test. When each grandson left for college, she typed a year's worth of prayers she'd prayed for him and mailed the list. While the boys were in college, she sent them weekly notes with a Bible verse and encouraging words. Nita knew that by the time the youngest was a senior, she'd be 80 years old, but she planned to pray as long as God gave her strength.

Here are some tips to get started if you'd like to organize a prayer group of your own.

Ask God to provide at least one other grandparent to join you. If you decide to make it a Grandmas In Touch group, part of the Moms In Touch International ministry, you can get a leader's guide and resources at momsintouch.org.

To help the others in the group know the grandkids they are praying for, have each person bring a three-ring notebook and a page with photos of each of her grandchildren with their names, ages and grade levels, schools, teachers if you want to include them, and city. That way, when a grandma is praying for a child she's never met, she can look at her photo to see what grade she's in and where she lives.

> ### It's a great honor and privilege
> for me to pray for my grandchildren. To know that I can be part of their struggles, joys, sadness, illness, protection, and so much more through my prayers is a great joy. Praying with other grandmas is the highlight of my week. In our group, we pray for one another's grandchildren using God's Word, which gives us confidence and hope. For example, we regularly pray for each child's salvation, placing their name in this verse: "I pray that Joshua will believe on the Lord Jesus Christ and be saved" (Acts 16:31). To hear another grandmother pray with such faith and love for my grandchild brings tears to my eyes and peace to my heart. And one by one our grandchildren are coming to know Christ.
>
> —Fern Nichols, Founder and President
> of Moms In Touch International

Instead of spending the hour hashing over problems, let me encourage you to talk more to God about the grandchildren than you do to each other.

Non-Material Blessings

Be assured that whether you pray for your grandkids in a group, with a prayer journal you present someday, through handprint prayers, or with a knitted prayer blanket, you will be passing on a legacy of blessing and love.

We give our grandchildren all kinds of gifts, but there is one gift that won't end up under a bunch of clutter in their closets or be sold in a garage sale.

It's a gift that won't put our bank account in the red and doesn't have to be charged on a credit card—yet it's worth more than anything material. Prayer is the gift that transcends time and space; it leaves a spiritual inheritance that will never fade away. Be encouraged when a prayer you've prayed for your grandkids might not be answered this year or next; all the prayers will, as E. M. Bounds said, "outlive your life and will shower your grandchildren with blessings long after your address has changed to heaven."

> ### Grandmothers who pray faithfully
> for their grandchildren give them the most precious gift that can be given—an invitation for God to do His work in the lives of those young ones.
>
> —Betty Southard & Jan Stoop

Chapter 17

The Best Gifts of All

Grandparents bestow upon their grandchildren
the strength and wisdom that time
and experience have given them.
Grandchildren bless their grandparents
with a youthful vitality and innocence
that help them stay young at heart forever.
Together they create a chain of love
linking the past with the future.
The chain may lengthen, but it will never part.

—Author Unknown

Our country seems to be filled with enthusiastic gift givers. Consumer research shows that during the 2007 Christmas season, people spent more than two hundred billion dollars on holiday purchases for their family and friends. Among them were a lot of grandparents, who now number over one third of the adult population.

As much as we love to give gifts to our darling grandkids, there are definitely challenges in the selection process. Sometimes a gift, though purchased with good intentions by the grandparents, can be a source of conflict with the parents. Problems also arise when grandparents use expensive gifts instead of time in a long-distance relationship, or when the parents think one child received more than another.

Sometimes a pair of grandparents, or multiples if there are blended families, unconsciously compete to see who can give the most elaborate gifts. A grandparent I know was upbraided by her son-in-law for giving bigger Christmas gifts than he and his wife could afford to give their child, making theirs look small and insignificant. In all of these cases, communication between the grown-ups can prevent a lot of problems. When in doubt, before buying a gift, ask the parents!

Sometimes a gift we have carefully thought about, shopped for, and purchased for our grandchild ends up as clutter on his or her closet floor or in the next garage sale.

Notebook Shopping

I'm continually amazed at the thoughtfulness of grandparents. A grandma in Illinois has had a tradition for many years called "Notebook Shopping" before each grandchild's birthday or Christmas. This wasn't a woman of great means, but she set aside money to do this for each child. An evening alone with Grandma was special in itself, but on these occasions the real issue was that Grandma was listening. The two would visit three stores; as they went up and down the aisles, the child pointed out items that attracted him while Grandma wrote them down in the notebook without assessment.

Later on during their dinner out together, she asked why the item appealed to him and followed up the conversation with questions designed to help her understand the grandchildren's thoughts and feelings. Future gifts were perhaps drawn from the list, but here's the catch—the grandchild knew that nothing was purchased on that trip. My five- and six-year-old grandsons might have a hard time with that idea! But hers knew way in advance this was the way Grandma's notebook shopping worked.

Once when this grandma was purchasing a gift from her notebook list, the clerk asked her what notebook shopping was, and Grandma explained. When the young woman responded, "I wish you'd adopt me!" Grandma agreed. She and the clerk made plans to meet at the mall the next week. The relationship has lasted for years and proved vital to a single college student with no extended family of her own.

And how did the grandchildren feel about the notebook shopping tradition? Even when they were in college, they still weren't ready to drop it. They loved the way their grandma cared enough to set aside a whole evening to hear their wants and feelings.

Special Choices and Time

Taking a grandchild out to a restaurant and a store seems to be a hit with most grandchildren. Kids appreciate special one-on-one time and love getting to choose their gifts. Mary Ann Edwards, my daughter-in-law Maggie's mom, invites each granddaughter out for a special dinner—any place they choose— and then takes her to pick out the outfit of her choice, with no parental or grandparental input allowed. The granddaughter also gets to pick whatever toy she

> It isn't the size of the gift that matters,
> but the size of the heart that gives it.
> —Eileen Elias Freeman

wants. What a celebration they have, just the two of them! For months ahead, the girls look forward to this time with Mimi.

Shirley, a Midwestern grandma, took each grandchild from the age of three out to lunch on his birthday and then to the store where he picked out a gift at a pre-set price. Those 13 grandchildren are now all grown and married, but to this day they want to have their birthday time with their grandmother. Now it's out for dinner—mates included.

Lisbeth and Stan Alexander gave the same thoughtful gift every year to their three grandchildren in Houston from the time they were five: a plane ticket to spend five days with the grandparents. One of their activities was—you've got it—a trip to the toy store to pick out their own gift. The grandkids felt very grown-up and special getting to fly and spend days being the only child in their grandparents' household.

Can you imagine as a kid being given a plane ticket and having one-on-one time with Grandma and Pop—plus a trip to a toy store? It must be a little like those TV programs in which the kid who wins a big contest gets to take a cart all around a toy store and put in everything he or she wants—but on a smaller scale. As a side note, I think the kids' parents were very trusting and cooperative to let their five- or six-year-olds fly alone—so kudos to them!

Creative Ideas for Gift-Giving

The 12 days of Christmas. Maria Cayere of Fairfax, Virginia, loves to find thoughtful gifts for her granddaughters Anna Maria and Emma, who live in Okinawa, Japan. At Christmastime, Maria buys 12 little gifts for Emma and Anna Maria, wraps each gift, and mails them. Cristina, their mom, puts the gifts under a small Christmas tree in the girls' room. Every night for 12 days before Christmas they get to open a little gift from Abi and Abo.

One night six-year-old Anna asked, "Daddy, do you think Abi is a fairy godmother?"

"Why do you think that?" her dad asked.

"Because I go to bed at night and dream about things I would like, and puff, the next day they are here in a package from Abi. I really think she's a fairy godmother!" The thoughtful gifts sent across the miles have let Anna and Emma know that Abi is thinking of them and loves them.

The gift of a collection. Patty thought long and hard about what kinds of gifts she wanted to give her grandsons. She believes that everyone needs a collection of some kind, so she decided to start her grandsons' collections from their cradle gifts on the occasion of their birth. Throughout their growing-up years on birthdays and Christmas, Patty bought an addition to the collection. It certainly made buying presents interesting for her. When Nathan, the oldest, was born, his baby gift was a fine grandfather clock. After that she bought him objects of art large and small. His wedding present was a large slab of petrified wood, which is becoming quite rare. Nathan has become a collector of artwork himself and bought his first painting just last year.

Nicholas's first present was a piece of fabric artwork Patty had commissioned for him. Over the years she's bought other quilts and hangings, including beaded ones done by fabric artists. For Zeb she began a coin collection. He now has a variety of coins in his collection, which adds to his appreciation of history. Joshua's birth present was a piece of the unique Spanish American art Patty had learned to love in New Mexico. When he came to visit his "Pabby," she began taking him to meet the artist who made the traditional Spanish art so he could pick out his own piece. The year he was 18 they went to a show of the works of Anita Romero Jones at a well-known gallery in Santa Fe. Josh got to talk to the artist and have his picture taken with her. The artist was happy to know that this handsome fellow was a collector of her work. Josh is very proud that he is a collector of Spanish American art, as are each of his brothers of their collections.

The gift of lessons or educational funds. If you're looking for meaningful ways to give gifts to your grandchildren, consider, after asking their parents, contributing to their college fund. Or perhaps you could pay for part of the music, tennis, or karate lessons they've always wanted to take and couldn't afford.

The gift of grandparenting other children. "Just because our grandchildren don't live close to us doesn't mean we can't have grandchildren in our daily lives," write Dr. Tim and Darcy Kimmel in *Extreme Grandparenting*. "There are families all around us who have children who could use some older, wiser people crossing their paths."

My dear friend Flo Perkins, who had a big bunch of grand- and great-grandchildren, was a surrogate grandparent for countless children in her Oklahoma City neighborhood for decades. And Clara, a Texas lady, is that kind of grandparent as well. She's marvelous to her brood, taking the grandchildren on Elderhostel trips and having them stay at her home, but she also "grandmothers" the kids in her neighborhood.

A retired teacher and the widow of a high school band director, Clara's relationship with one of those children began when she offered to give him music lessons when he was in elementary school. Now he is about to begin his senior year; and one of the highlights of the past few summers has been going with Clara to volunteer at a nearby hospital. She rounds up the neighborhood kids, they board the metro bus, and off they go. She has them signed up, trained, and committed in no time. They learn to serve by working side by side with her. Her influence has been felt in the lives of countless children who needed a loving grandparent, as well as in the lives of the hospital patients she helps the kids bless.

The Gift of Good Memories

One of my heroes is Mimi, my husband's mom. Here's how our daughter Ali describes her grandma and you'll see why she's the kind of grandparent I want to be.

My favorite memories of Mimi are renting movies together, sometimes watching two in a row and staying up super late. I saw Gone With the Wind *with Mimi and some other great old movies. She'd even watch Nickelodeon (a kids' channel) with me for as long as I wanted. It was such a treat and so fun that she wanted to do what I thought was fun, even though it might have been boring to her. I never knew; I just felt so at ease sharing my excitement with her over little things I loved.*

Mimi's gift-giving was, yes, super nice—I loved going to the Wal-Mart in their little town of Pawhuska. But what stands out the most is that when I'd get to go and spend time with her, she would ask me what I wanted to do, then we'd do it. She'd get my favorite food and act like she was having a blast eating whatever I picked. She knew I loved special trips to Eskimo Joe's in Stillwater, so sometimes we'd just jump in the car and go, footloose and fancy free. I really appreciated her ease in spending time together. No agenda, no pretenses; she just listened a lot. Now I see that Mimi was a "spend time" person, that she just enjoyed being together. She was very giving and unselfish in sharing time with me. I always felt at ease because she made fun with her so easy—even at times in my life when I felt I didn't fit at school or was struggling with something. It made me feel very special.

The Best Gifts of All

Of all the wonderful gifts we can give our grandkids, some of the best aren't as much about money as the time we spend with them and our involvement in their lives: the gift of good memories enjoyed together at holiday gatherings, Cousin Camps, or a shared trip.

I love what Cindi Plum said about giving the gift of a Christmas trip rather than an expensive electronic toy.

This generation of kids gets a lot of stuff; I'd rather have time together with our grandsons Noah and Luke on a memory-making trip: tubing on a snowy Colorado hill, snowball fights, hot cocoa and games we play together at night. That's going to last much longer than a toy that's soon forgotten or broken.

What will our grandkids remember? Reading books and cooking together. The way we listen to their joys and pains.

Taking a walk in the woods together on a cold December day. Going to the movies together, or becoming pen pals via the postal service or e-mail. Memory scrapbooks and photos that connect us across the miles. Sharing our interests and passions; it might be a passion for sports or baking, history or art, but when we take the time to pass it on to our grandchild, it deepens the connection we have. These are all gifts of time, involvement, and love that will last a lifetime.

Passing It On

We were meant to give our lives away.
Spend more time living your legacy
instead of worrying about leaving it.

—Lee J. Colan

Relationship-building is a process that happens slowly over time. As we've seen in the stories in this book, it's the small, loving things we do through the years that build the grandparent-grandchild connection: singing a lullaby and rocking them when they're babies; blowing bubbles to hear that belly laugh when they're toddlers; going to the zoo together and eating pancakes at the local waffle shop—just the two of us; showing up at milestones like graduations; sending cards of encouragement; and all the hugs, smiles, and phone calls in between through elementary school, high school, and college.

The miles may separate us from our grandchildren, and certainly as they grow, the busyness of their lives will increase, but we can provide the unconditional love and acceptance that they need to grow and face the challenges ahead. That's a gift that will last. I love how Marsha Van puts it: "Their parents are busy creating good citizens, but while we reinforce the same values, our main goal is to shower the grandkids with love and affection. Like a soft feather bed, we give them comfort and encouragement."

When divorce, death, or moving brings change and uncertainty to our grandchildren's lives, we can give the gift of a safe place and sense of security. The loving relationship we've built steadies them when the inevitable storms come. As grandparents, we're an important source of continuity, communicated through holiday traditions, customs, faith, and family history, creating a chain of love linking the past with the future.

> Grandparents are truly the best way to teach history to children, because they are living historians and your connection to the past.
>
> —Willard Scott

As we pass on our heritage and values through the stories we tell, grandchildren receive the gift of belonging and begin to understand that they aren't alone. They are part of a family whose roots go deep; as an old song says, "We're a family and we're a tree, our roots go deep down in history, from my great-great-granddaddy reaching up to me; we're a green and growing family tree." Through our stories we pass on positive, enduring values to the next generation.

Most importantly, our prayers can surround our grandchildren all the way from the cradle to college and beyond, providing wind beneath their wings as they embark on their adult lives and build their own families. Our prayers are one of the greatest gifts because they don't fade, rust, or go away. They continue showering our grandkids' lives with blessings even when we've graduated to heaven.

As grandparents, we can also give the gift of a good example and model a life of meaning, hope, and service to others. As they see us take care of ourselves and stay energetic into old age, they won't worry about us as much! Seeing us continuing to be active and have purpose encourages them about the future they can't see, just as their energy and youthfulness inspires us.

We aren't perfect grandparents and things don't always go the way we hope they will. Often there are factors beyond our control. Sometimes we blow it and other times our "grand" plans get derailed despite our best efforts. Divorce or an overseas move may separate us for a time. And sometimes we suffer with illness or are just plain tired.

> The time you spend with your grandchildren today gives them memories that will last forever.
>
> —Audrey Sherins

As Phyllis Stanley wrote to me, "Like you, we love our grandchildren so much and thank God for the privilege of being involved in their lives. I understand well the weariness and medical problems and sometimes the criticism for the life that we try to pour out. But, we don't give in and we don't give up—we're called to be life-givers and even in our weakness and not doing things as others would like, we press on for as long as God gives us strength." As we do, it makes a difference in our grandkids' lives, not just in this season but for the long term.

It is a difficult world to be growing up in. But throughout history we see that, even in the most challenging circumstances, children can achieve and make great contributions to their world when they know that someone believes in them and loves them no matter what. What a privilege to be that person in their lives! What a marvelous thing it is to get to be a grandparent! And what a blessing and gift our grandsons and granddaughters are to us.

My hope is that the stories in this book have inspired you and that the ideas and tips will give you lots of resources to connect during the different stages and seasons of life, wherever your grandkids live. Enjoy them whenever you can—for just as our children's messy little fingerprints on the wall got higher and higher until they were gone, our grandkids will grow up quickly.

About the Author

Cheri Fuller is a popular speaker and best-selling author of 40 books with combined sales of over one million, including *The One Year Women's Friendship Devotional, A Busy Woman's Guide to Prayer, The One Year Book of Praying Through the Bible*, her award-winning book, *The Mom You're Meant to Be*, and others. A wife, mother, and grandmother to six lively grandchildren, Cheri's greatest joy has been building families and helping parents unlock their kids' learning and spiritual potential as we leave a great legacy of faith to the next generation. Now she has embarked on a mission to inspire grandparents all across the country to connect heart to heart with their grandkids.

Cheri, a former Oklahoma Mother of the Year, speaks to women at many retreats and conferences. She's written magazine articles and Internet columns that provide hope and encouragement to people throughout the U.S. and other countries. She was an education writer for *Family Circle* magazine, is a contributing writer for *Today's Christian Woman* and *ParentLife*, and a regular contributor to *Focus on the Family* and other publications. Her Web site, www.cherifuller.com, includes the column "Mothering By Heart," Bible studies and book guides, plus her eNewsletter, which goes to hundreds of women throughout the world.

Cheri and her husband, Holmes, live in Oklahoma. They have three grown and married children and six grandchildren who bring great joy to their lives.

FOCUS ON THE FAMILY®

Welcome to the Family

Whether you purchased this book, borrowed it, or received it as a gift, thanks for reading it! This is just one of many insightful, biblically based resources that Focus on the Family produces for people in all stages of life.

Focus is a global Christian ministry dedicated to helping families thrive as they celebrate and cultivate God's design for marriage and experience the adventure of parenthood. Our outreach exists to support individuals and families in the joys and challenges they face, and to equip and empower them to be the best they can be.

Through our many media outlets, we offer help and hope, promote moral values and share the life-changing message of Jesus Christ with people around the world.

Focus on the Family MAGAZINES

These faith-building, character-developing publications address the interests, issues, concerns, and challenges faced by every member of your family from preschool through the senior years.

For More INFORMATION

 ONLINE:
Log on to
FocusOnTheFamily.com
In Canada, log on to
FocusOnTheFamily.ca

 PHONE:
Call toll-free:
**800-A-FAMILY
(232-6459)**
In Canada, call toll-free:
800-661-9800

| **THRIVING FAMILY™**
Marriage & Parenting | **FOCUS ON THE FAMILY CLUBHOUSE JR.®**
Ages 4 to 8 | **FOCUS ON THE FAMILY CLUBHOUSE®**
Ages 8 to 12 | **FOCUS ON THE FAMILY CITIZEN®**
U.S. news issues |

Rev. 10/10

More Great Resources
from Focus on the Family®

Extreme Grandparenting
by Tim and Darcy Kimmel
Make the most of your role as grandparent—a role being redefined today by active, vital grandparents like you. The honesty, humor, stories, and practical experience offered will motivate and guide you to develop richer relationships with your children and their children. *Extreme Grandparenting* encourages you to give the greatest gift possible to family: yourself.

Your Spouse Isn't the Person You Married: Keeping Love Strong Through Life's Changes
by Teri K. Reisser, MFT and Paul C. Reisser, MD
Using candid insights, humor, and stories drawn from years of experience, the Reissers show how to prevent and repair marriage rifts that develop with time. Recapture intimacy and grow closer to your spouse—not further apart.

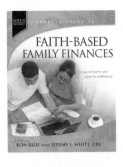

Complete Guide to Faith-Based Family Finances
by Ron Blue and Jeremy White
Whether you're a financial whiz, a financial novice, or somewhere in between, the *Complete Guide to Faith-Based Family Finances* is filled with commonsense, practical tools to help you make wise financial decisions year after year. In addition to covering every area of financial planning, this helpful resource contains the answers to many of the questions asked by families like yours.

FOR MORE INFORMATION

Online:
Log on to FocusOnTheFamily.com
In Canada, log on to FocusOnTheFamily.ca

 Phone:
Call toll-free: 800-A-FAMILY
In Canada, call toll-free: 800-661-9800

BPZZXP1

Special Notes about My Grandkids

Special Notes about My Grandkids

Special Notes about My Grandkids

Special Notes about My Grandkids

Special Notes about My Grandkids

Special Notes about My Grandkids

Special Notes about My Grandkids

Special Notes about My Grandkids

Special Notes about My Grandkids